INTERACTIVE ART WORKSHOP

Set Your Mixed Media in Motion

Kim Rae Nugent

NORTH LIGHT BOOKS
Cincinnati, Ohio

www.mycraftivity.com

Published by North Light Books, an imprint of F+W Publications, Inc., 4700 East Galbraith Road, Cincinnati, Ohio 45236. (800) 289-0963. First edition.

12 11 10 09 08   5 4 3 2 1

Distributed in Canada by Fraser Direct
100 Armstrong Avenue
Georgetown, ON, Canada L7G 5S4
Tel: (905) 877-4411

Distributed in the U.K. and Europe by David & Charles
Brunel House, Newton Abbot, Devon, TQ12 4PU, England
Tel: (+44) 1626 323200, Fax: (+44) 1626 323319
E-mail: postmaster@davidandcharles.co.uk

Distributed in Australia by Capricorn Link
P.O. Box 704, S. Windsor, NSW 2756 Australia
Tel: (02) 4577-3555

Library of Congress Cataloging-in-Publication Data
Nugent, Kim Rae.
Interactive art workshop : set your mixed media in motion / Kim Rae Nugent. -- 1st ed.
p. cm.
Includes index.
ISBN 978-1-60061-080-6 (alk. paper)
1. Handicraft. 2. Interactive art. I. Title.
TT157.N84 2008
745.5--dc22

2008017566

Editor: Robin M. Hampton
Designer: Geoff Raker
Cover Designer: Stephanie Goodrich
Production Coordinator: Greg Nock
Photographers: John Carrico, Alias Imaging LLC; Adam Hand; Christine Polomsky

About the Author

Kim Rae Nugent is a mixed-media artist and teacher who enjoys working in collage, oil painting, sculpture, sewing, altered books and assemblage. Kim has studied art at the University of Wisconsin–Milwaukee, University of Wisconsin–Washington County and Cardinal Stritch University. Her artwork has been featured in several Stampington & Co. publications and in *Artist Trading Card Workshop*, published by North Light Books. Kim is an active member of the Cedarburg Artists Guild and participates regularly in local and national exhibits and shows.

Metric Conversion Chart

to convert	to	multiply by
Inches	Centimeters	2.54
Centimeters	Inches	0.4
Feet	Centimeters	30.5
Centimeters	Feet	0.03
Yards	Meters	0.9
Meters	Yards	1.1
Sq. Inches	Sq. Centimeters	6.45
Sq. Centimeters	Sq. Inches	0.16
Sq. Feet	Sq. Meters	0.09
Sq. Meters	Sq. Feet	10.8
Sq. Yards	Sq. Meters	0.8
Sq. Meters	Sq. Yards	1.2
Pounds	Kilograms	0.45
Kilograms	Pounds	2.2
Ounces	Grams	28.3
Grams	Ounces	0.035

www.fwpublications.com

Dedication

This book is dedicated:
To my father, Ken Hollnagel. He was a very talented craftsman who could accomplish any project that he set his mind to. I am grateful to both of my parents, who raised me to be without fear of trying to achieve my heart's desires.

To Granny Eleanore, my muse for paper arts.

To my children, Brook, Aren and Casey. Through imagination and creativity, I wish you wings to fly.

Butterfly Card
Gail Suhfras

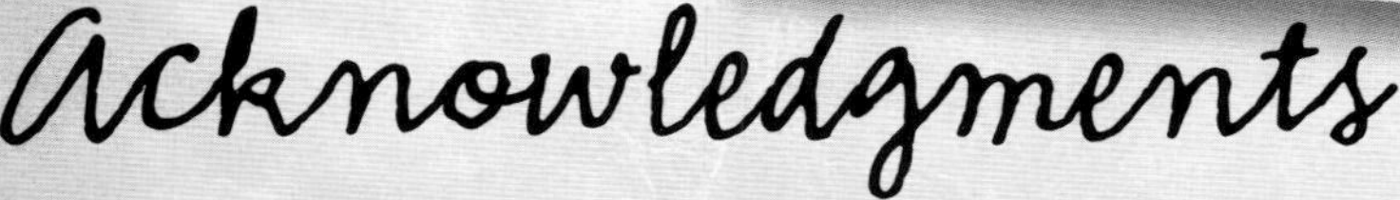

Acknowledgments

I would like to thank my friend Bernie Berlin, who always has a plethora of ideas. Her example inspired me and showed me that it is possible to write a how-to book for artists. Bernie is always willing to share what she has learned and is my information highway.

Thank you to all of the contributing artists. It was challenging for you to contribute projects without seeing the book, and the book wouldn't be what it is without your contributions. You have amazed me with your brilliant art. Special thanks to my friend Gail Suhfras, my muse for dedication, patience and perserverance.

To my husband, Mark, thank you for supporting me and the children all of these years. It is not easy living with an artist and her abundance of ideas, many of which require your craftsmanship, ingenuity and hard work.

To my mom, Joan, thank you for providing me with an artful life. It is because of you that I grew up in idyllic surroundings filled with whimsy, inspiration, plentiful art supplies and an artist to emulate.

To my younger sister, Jodi, you proved to me years ago that it is possible to make a living as an artist, and I have a great admiration for your work.

To my son-in-law, Joel, thank you for supporting me by modeling for some of my crazy ideas.

Thank you to the Eastern Shores Library System. You fostered my love of how-to books and assisted me in many projects throughout my life, including this book. As a young mother with three children, you provided a haven. We could leave the library feeling rich, each carrying a pile of books.

Finally, thank you to the staff at F+W Publications: Tonia Davenport, my acquisitions editor, for believing in and promoting the book that I proposed; Robin Hampton, my editor, for her guidance, support and chocolate; and Christine Polomsky, the talented photographer who makes her job look easy.

Altered Amusements
Jill Marie Shulse

Contents

To my Sweetheart
Secrets of the Se

Introduction

When you read a novel, your senses are activated through your imagination. When you look at a picture book, you're treated to visual imagery through an artist's eyes. When you're handling an interactive book, it's a hands-on experience beckoning you to participate in the story. As a child I was fascinated by the way interactive books worked, and I still am—pulling tabs, spinning circles, lifting flaps and touching textural images—how fun! But, I've always found it more enjoyable to re-create these mechanisms in my own art than to simply be content with the original book. As I've grown as an artist, so has my appreciation for interactive techniques. No longer limited to children's art, they're now quite sophisticated in style and message.

There are two basic approaches to creating interactive art, and you'll learn both in this book: You can use existing artwork and add interactive mechanisms to it. *To My Sweetheart* (page 14) and *Eagle's Enigma* (page 18) are both examples of this method. This approach allows you to explore an idea further and reinvent your work. Or, you can create the mechanism and then apply the art. *Magnetic Personality* (page 40) and *Roar of the Lion* (page 78) are two models of this approach. Much of the artwork in this book features an amalgamation of both approaches.

I have many aspirations for my own interactive artwork. Sometimes, I want my art to make viewers smile, chuckle or laugh. At times, I wish to inspire with a serious message. Often, I just want to create something beautiful. If you like to experiment with various techniques and styles as much as I do, you'll be amazed at how far you can go once your work becomes interactive. But the inspiration for an interactive piece doesn't have to be interactive itself. Picasso inspired the cover of my *Colorful Characters* album (page 109) and the *Circle Flip* project (page 98). In antiques shops, try searching for mechanical or movable vintage greeting cards and postcards. Some of the mechanisms are brilliant. The idea for *Squeaker Mouse* (page 102) came from a vintage postcard of a cat with a squeaker inside. The inspiration for *To My Sweetheart* (page 14) was an antique valentine. If you want to explore an idea or style further, try combining several interactive elements into a book as I've done in the *Secrets of the Sea* (cover shown at left) and *Colorful Characters* (cover shown on page 109).

Alongside my own work, in these pages you'll find inspiring artwork from more than twenty contributing artists. As you look, you'll find their amazing pieces of art that virtually any artist's style can be enhanced with the use of interactive elements. Joan E. Hollnagel's work (pages 19, 35 and 114) combines a whimsical style with sophisticated technique. Jill K. Berry's work (pages 29, 43, 52, 101, 105, 109, 112 and 116) is as precise and well constructed as it is beautiful. Jill Marie Shulse's work (page 117) is incredibly complex with layers of meaning and interactive elements combined.

You're sure to find countless possibilities for the techniques demonstrated in this book to apply to your own work. You'll learn to set your art in motion with pivots, pull tabs, rotating wheels, secret flaps and more. A great technique to start with is the simple method of recycling a plastic puzzle (page 33). For more of a challenge, try the Revolving Picture technique (page 68). It's the most complex mechanism, but it's well worth the effort. Soon, you'll be inspired to include many mechanisms in a single piece of art. Get creative and get moving!

What You Need

Most interactive projects can be completed with a small selection of tools. After all, it's better to spend your time creating art rather than just collecting more and more tools and supplies.

Looking Sharp

For the best results, use sharp cutting instruments when creating interactive mechanisms.

Cutting Tools

A personal trimmer with a scoring blade is the must-have tool to give your art a neat, professional appearance. Cutting straight lines is essential for constructing interactive mechanisms that work properly, and the scoring blade helps you create precise folds.

Scissors create a variety of cuts for interactive art—use crafting scissors for cutting paper and fabric, precision-tip scissors for cutting small details and decorative scissors for creating graspable edges on movable wheels.

A cutting mat protects your surface when using a craft knife or setting eyelets.

A craft knife makes precise cuts around shapes. Use a sharp blade to make cutting easier and to prevent jagged edges.

Wire cutters are the best tool for cutting wires used in interactive mechanisms. Don't use scissors to cut wires; it dulls blades.

Shaping Tools

An eyelet tool set and a hammer make holes for eyelets, brads or fibers (or whatever you decide to attach to your art) and to set the eyelets in place. A small hammer is sufficient for use with the eyelet tool set.

A compass or template creates a variety of circles, which is useful for making mechanical parts.

Rulers and straightedges enable you to draw straight lines.

A circle punch or gasket punch set works well for making small circles and comes in a variety of sizes. Borrow the gasket punch set from a mechanic's tool chest to create circles where a circle punch can't reach.

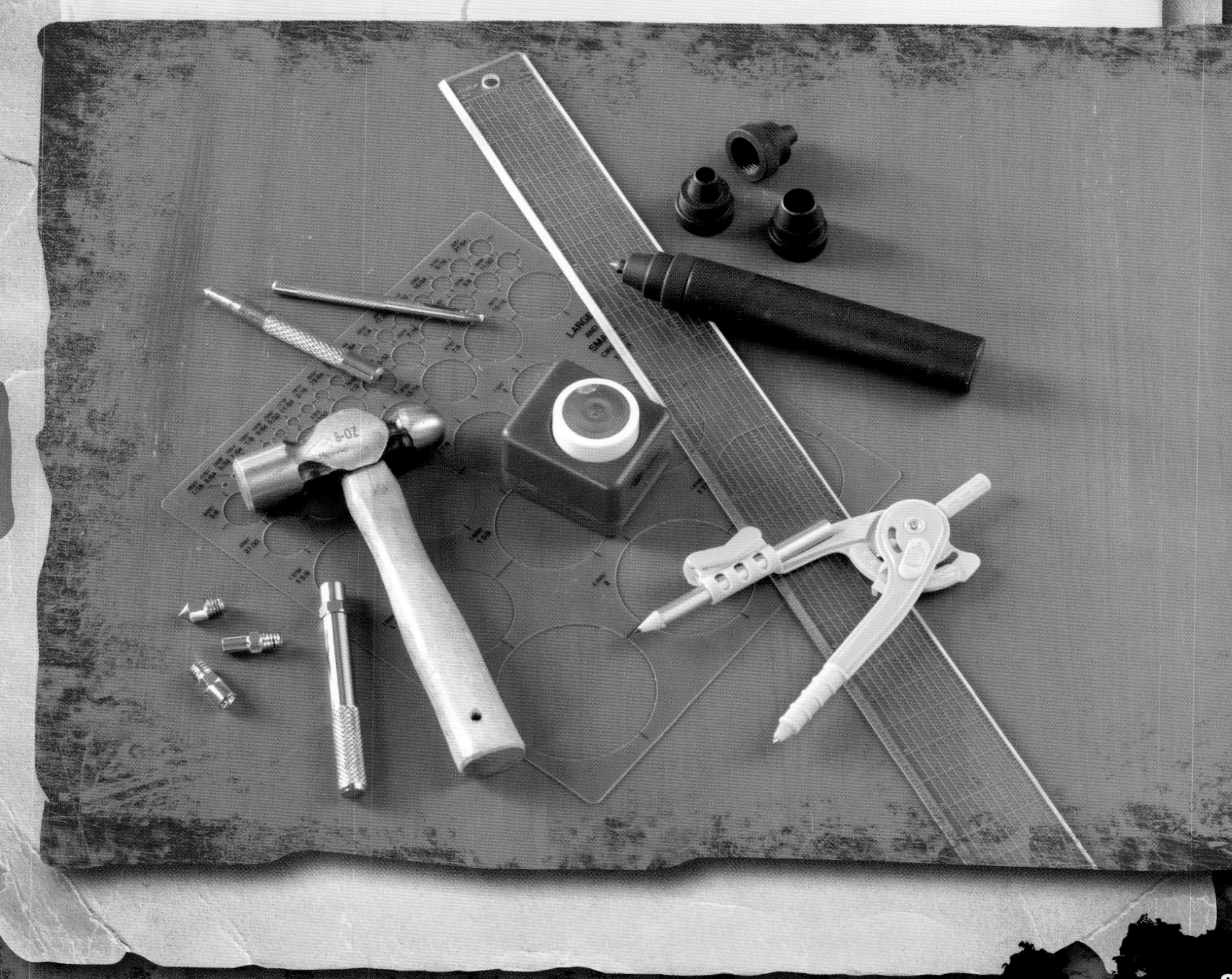

Art Supplies

Heavyweight cardstock is essential to creating interactive mechanisms that will hold up to repeated use. [It comes in various weights, but I recommend 80 lb. (170 grams).]

Pens, pencils, pastels, paints and paintbrushes allow you to create a rich and colorful palette. Some of my favorite mediums are water-soluble oil pastels and oil paint sticks.

Watercolor paper accepts a variety of wet and dry mediums. [It comes in various weights, but I recommend 140 lb. (300 grams).]

Bristol paper with its smooth finish makes an excellent surface for pen and ink. [It comes in various weights, but I recommend 100 lb. (210 grams).]

Adhesives and Fasteners

E-6000 adhesive works great for adhering three-dimensional items.

Water-based dimensional adhesive works well to adhere paper to plastic.

Glue sticks work well for adhering paper with a matte surface. Be sure to choose a glue stick that is permanent.

Permanent double-stick tape or adhesive rollers are fast, without the problem of wrinkles.

All-purpose glue is useful for adhering paper, but be aware that it has a tendency to wrinkle when used on lighter-weight papers.

Fasteners, such as eyelets, brads, wire and string, can be used in a variety of ways in your interactive projects. Keep an assortment of sizes in your basic tool kit.

Interactive Supplies

Squeakers and bells provide an easy way to add sound to your art.

Silk flowers, self-adhesive gemstones and ribbons make your art a tactile experience.

Perfumes, spices and unflavored drink mixes create pleasing scents that can be used in scratch-n-sniff projects.

Puzzles add movement in a fun, interactive way.

To my Sweetheart

Chapter 1

Turning Points

Spin, revolve and swing: These are a few of the functions a pivoting mechanism can accomplish. In this chapter, you'll learn several ways to set your mixed media in pivoting motion. We'll start simply by using brads to attach pivoting parts to a work of art (page 14). Not only are these pivots easy to make, they also allow you to assemble and disassemble your art to work out the design details. Once you've mastered the basics, we'll challenge you to move on to more permanent pivots, such as using an eyelet to articulate a portion of a picture—or, in my example, several eyelets to really bring a piece of art to life (page 26). Then we'll move on to creating a revolving wheel that can change the look of an entire piece with a simple spin (pages 20 and 24).

To My Sweetheart

Brad Pivot

Brads are useful tools for creating pivoting mechanisms. You can easily attach and remove them while working out the details of your artwork. Brads are available in different sizes and finishes; some even have decorative heads that can be incorporated into a design. You can use these pivots to add movement or to reveal hidden pieces within your work.

Moving art

Attaching multiple copies of a photo with a brad provides an easy, interactive component to your work by creating a layer that will remain stationary and an additional layer that moves. In this example, swinging Mary Margaret's arms from side to side causes her eyes to move, too. Dancing legs, waving arms or a wagging tail are just some of the possibilities of movement you can give to your subject.

Materials

- image
- cardstock
- personal trimmer with a scoring blade
- scissors
- craft knife
- cutting mat
- glue stick
- brad
- pencil

optional materials

- silk flowers
- water-based dimensional adhesive

Prepare photos

Size the photograph to the desired size using a computer or a copier. Make a minimum of 2 copies of the photo. Using photo 1, cut around the portion of the photo that will remain stationary (here, it's the legs, skirt and body).

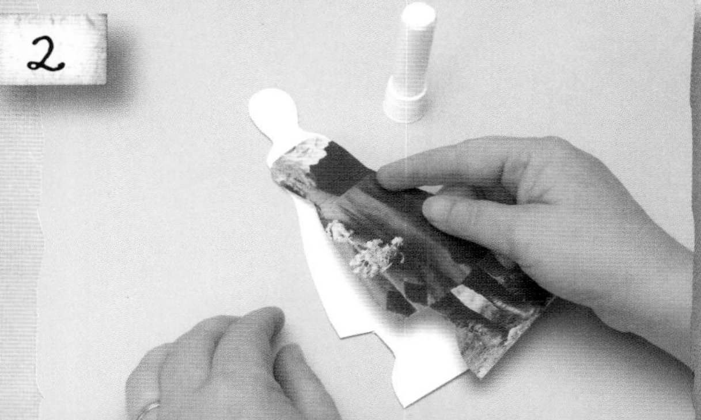

Adhere to cardstock

Trace the image's shape from photo 1 onto cardstock. Include a shape for under the movable piece (which i've decided will be the head), but make it smaller than the actual head piece in the photo. (This is where the pupils will be drawn.) Adhere photo 1 to the cardstock. This is now your project piece.

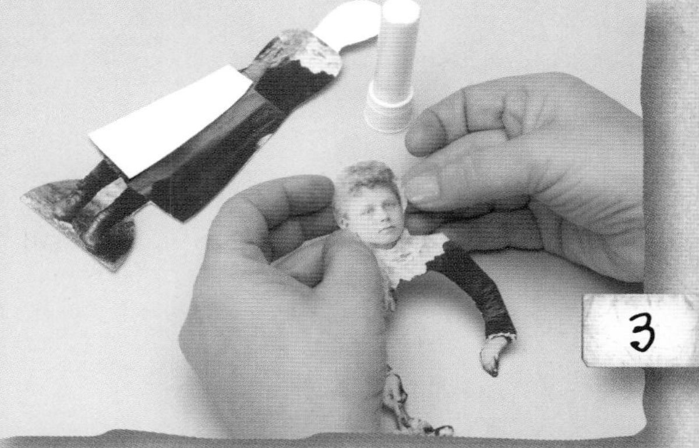

Cover photo 1

Cut from photo 2 the portion that will move (here, the head, arms and basket). Keep this piece for use in step 4. Remove a portion from photo 2 to cover the stationary parts of the project piece (shown in white for instructional purposes). Add a section of hair cut from photo 1 to the right side of the moving head piece to allow the mechanism to move without exposing the underlying piece.

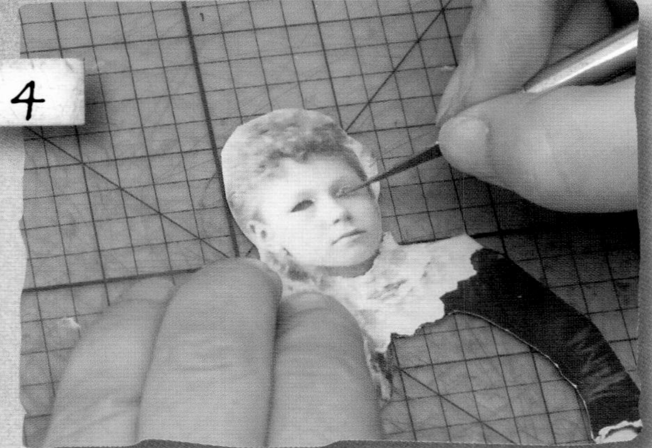

Cut openings for eyes

Place the piece that will be movable on a cutting mat. Cut openings with a sharp craft knife where you would like to create an interactive effect. Here, I'm cutting eye openings in my head piece.

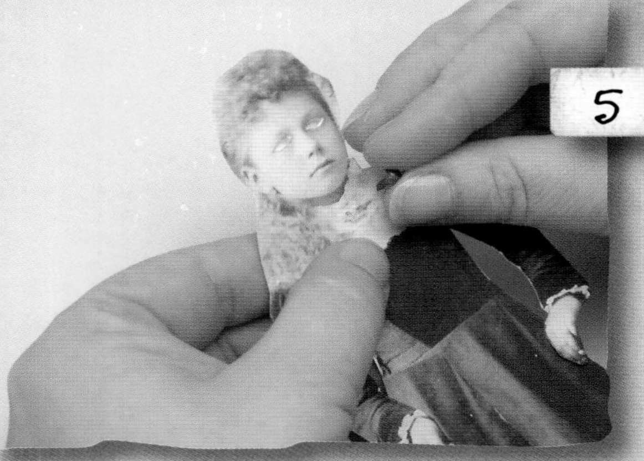

Attach upper body

Lay the upper body piece from step 4 over the project piece so the shoulders line up. Use a craft knife to make a small slit in the center of the neck, cutting through the upper body piece and the project piece. Insert a brad in the slit through both layers. Flip the project over and spread the back of the brad to attach.

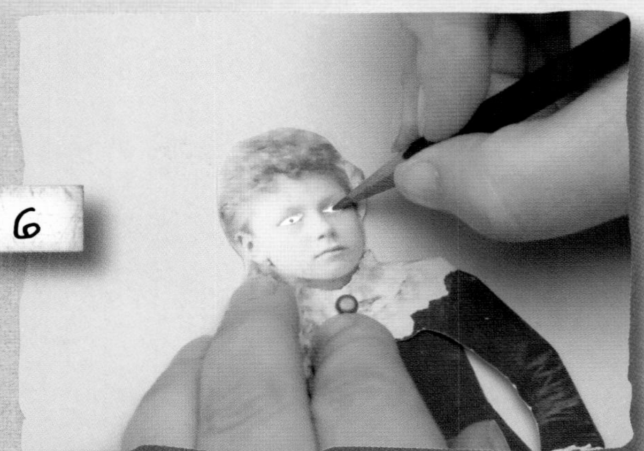

Mark pupils

Make sure the pivot pieces are aligned and add the element you'd like to appear to move to the bottom layer. Here, I'm using a pencil to make small marks in the center of the eye slits to indicate pupils.

Draw irises

Flip the project to the back. Fold in the ends of the brad. Remove the brad. Remove the movable piece from the project piece and complete the element you began in step 6. Here, I'm drawing irises on the project piece using the pupils drawn in step 6 as my center point. Reassemble the figure and test the mechanism. Here, I can now swing the arms from side to side to move the eyes from side to side in the openings. Trim excess cardstock from the project piece if needed.

Attach paper stop

Cut a strip from cardstock that's ¼" (6mm) wide and slightly longer than the width of the movable piece. Fold the outer ends of the strip over. The strip should now be slightly smaller than the width of the movable piece. Slide the tabs of the paper strip between the movable piece and the cardstock. Glue the strip in place, taking care not to cover the openings with the folded tabs. Cut the tabs if necessary.

Embellish with flowers and note (optional)

Complete your piece however you'd like. I decided to adhere the silk flowers to the basket with a water-based dimensional adhesive. I then created an envelope for my subject to hold and adhered it with a glue stick.

Create stand

Cut a triangle shape from cardstock that's about ½ the length of the project and ½ the width of the project. My stand was 3" × 1½" (8cm × 4cm). Using a personal trimmer, score about ¼" (6mm) from the vertical side of the triangle.

Attach stand

Place the triangle, centered on the back of the project and aligned with the bottom. Place glue on the ¼" (6mm) section and adhere it to the project. Fold the stand so it supports the project.

Hidden art

A brad pivot makes it possible to incorporate hidden treasures in your artwork by creating a pivoting cover. Pieces that are similar, yet still distinct, take well to this technique. In *Eagle's Enigma* (starting on this page), articulating the wing allowed me to completely cover and uncover the hand of this anthropomorphic eagle. Think about a message that you would like to reveal in your art.

Eagle's Enigma

rotate my wing

Materials

- image
- second image
- scissors
- glue stick
- brad
- eyelet tool set and hammer

Out of sight

If you don't like the look of brad heads in your art, you can easily hide them by sandwiching the brad between two pieces of paper.

1

Prepare images

Make 2 copies of the image of the part you want to move (I've chosen a wing): 1 to use as your project piece, and 1 to move and reveal something underneath. Cut a third image (I've chosen a hand) to place under the pivot piece.

2

Cover photo 1

From photo 2, cut a piece that you want to move and some background pieces. Cut a piece for the underside of the movable piece if you want to hide the brad. Use a glue stick to adhere the background to cover your project piece.

Attach photo 2

Lay the image that you want hidden on the project piece to test for placement. Lay the pivot piece over the image and test the movement to determine its pivot point. Use a glue stick to adhere the hand. With an eyelet tool and hammer make a hole at the pivot point in the project piece. Make a corresponding hole in the underside of the pivot piece.

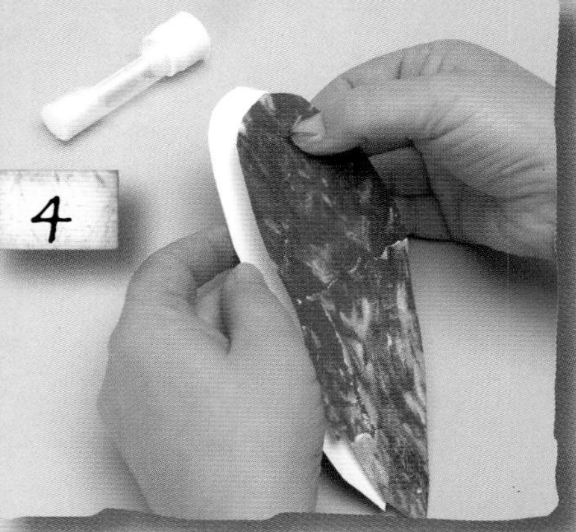

Insert brad

Place the brad through the hole on the movable piece. If you want to hide the brad, place the brad through the second piece you cut out in step 2, and glue the upper wing to the under wing, sandwiching the brad head between.

Attach movable piece

Place the movable piece with the brad through the hole on the project piece and turn it over. Spread the back of the brad to secure it.

Nesting Bird
Gina Louthian-Stanley

Birds
Brook W. Berth

Girl Sitting in Chair
Joan E. Hollnagel

As the Wheel Turns

Wheel Pivot

Put a spin on your own ideas by turning a wheel to change pictures within a frame. Depending upon the size of the wheel and the size of the opening, you can present several different rotating pictures. Use this technique to showcase distinct images, as in *As the Wheel Turns*; or create an image that morphs into something new as you turn the wheel, as in *Fashion Show* (page 24).

Materials

- heavyweight watercolor paper
- scissors
- decorative scissors
- craft knife
- cutting mat
- glue stick
- brad
- eyelet tool set and hammer
- compass
- pencil

optional materials

- magazine images
- metal tape
- oil paint sticks
- plastic template

Changing image

Featuring a smaller opening allows you to highlight several images. In this example, I chose a rectangular picture frame to define my opening. There is an infinite variety of shapes possible. Contemplate the different objects represented by a circle, square or free-form shape. Use this technique when you need multiple images to tell the story or to indicate many choices. Here Eddie sits back and contemplates, *What is art*?

1

Prepare background

Paint, draw or use a photo for your background image. I used oil paint sticks to add more detail and color in the background.

Scissor Savvy

When starting a new cut using decorative scissors, line the teeth up with the previous cut. Don't close the scissors completely, or the paper will tear.

2

Create wheel

Mark a wheel that's slightly smaller than your image using a compass. Cut out the wheel with decorative scissors to create a graspable edge. Punch a hole in the center of the wheel with a hammer and eyelet tool set.

3

Mark pivot point

Place the turning wheel on the back of the page, extending it past 1 of the edges. Mark a pivot point with a pencil on the turning wheel and the back of the page.

Attach small circle

Cut a circle approximately 2½" (6cm) in diameter and punch a hole in the center. Place a brad in the hole and adhere the circle to the back of the picture, placing the brad over the pivot mark. Let it dry. This circle allows you to pivot the wheel without having the brad show through the other side of the page.

Create frame

Cut an opening in the center of the tape with a sharp craft knife to create a frame where you want the the rotating images to appear. Take care to design the opening so it doesn't extend past the edge of where the turning wheel will be. I used metal tape for my frame.

Circle Turn
Sandra McCutcheon Pape

The Seer
Barbe Saint John

Open Your Eyes
Hope M. Clinchot

Mark openings for art

Attach the turning wheel with a brad where you marked the pivot points in step 3. Turn the project over and mark a rectangle opening on the circle with a pencil. Rotate the wheel until the drawn rectangle disappears and mark another one. Repeat this step until you come to the first rectangle drawn.

Attach and embellish art

Remove the turning wheel and use a glue stick to adhere a piece of art in each shape. I made a template of plastic and placed it over magazine images to find portions that I found appealing. I then used the paint sticks to highlight the art.

Shaping up

Experiment with different shapes for your opening. The possibilities are endless.

change my color

Chameleon
Kim Rae Nugent

Continuous Image

Sometimes you want your design to seem to morph into a new design or color scheme. To accomplish this, draw or apply one continuous image on the rotating circle. For *Fashion Show*, I created an interesting variety of forms and shapes using a pipette and ink. As you turn the wheel, numerous possibilities for her dress design appear. Use this technique when you want to create a kaleidoscope effect.

Fashion Show

give me a new dress

Materials

- cardstock
- Bristol paper
- craft knife
- cutting mat
- brad
- eyelet tool set and hammer
- compass
- pencil

optional materials

- ink
- pipette
- markers
- decorative scissors

Tips

- The diameter of the wheel should be less than the width of your project.
- The wheel should extend past one side of your project piece so you can turn it.
- Consider where your pivot point will fall on your design. If you're using a transparency, as I did here, is it in a place where the transparency will be?

1

Start image

Use a compass to create a circle that is slightly smaller than the outer piece on heavyweight watercolor paper. Hand tear or use decorative scissors to cut out the circle. Pick any place on the wheel to start drawing or painting your image.

2

Turn and continue

Continue to turn the rotating wheel while applying your design to the entire surface. I used a pipette. Let the design dry, if needed.

3

Color image (optional) and attach

If desired, fill your design with color. Punch a hole in the center of the wheel with a hammer and eyelet tool set. Place the turning wheel on the back of the page, extending it past 1 of the edges. Mark a pivot point with a pencil. Attach the wheel to the project piece with an eyelet or brad.

move all my legs
Catch of the Day Isn't Always What It's Cracked Up to Be

Eyelet Pivot

An ideal way to articulate an object is to add eyelets as pivoting mechanisms where the joints are located. The advantage to using eyelets is that they lay flatter than brad heads and are neater in appearance than brad legs on the back of the piece. The downside to using eyelets is that they are relatively permanent once they are in place.

I went a bit overboard when I chose a lobster to illustrate this technique. The exoskeleton of this animal provided a challenging way for me to experiment with eyelet pivots. Although the lobster as a whole seems complex, each joint mechanism is easily produced.

Materials

- cardstock
- scissors
- glue stick
- eyelets
- eyelet tool set and hammer
- cutting mat
- pencil

optional materials

- magazine images
- elastic cord
- fiber
- oil paint sticks

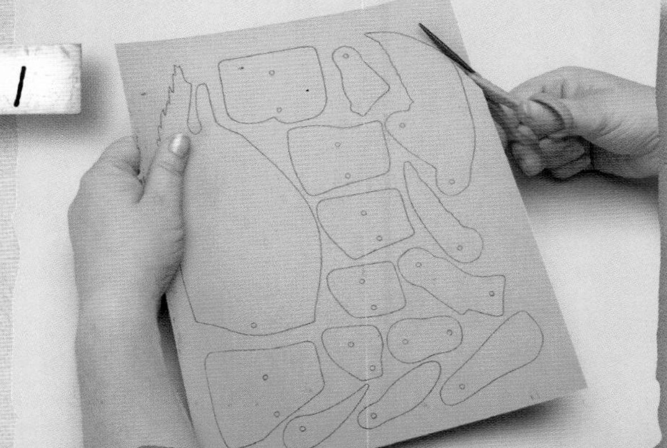

Prepare photo

Draw a subject with many movable parts onto a piece of cardstock. Cut the copy into individual pieces to be articulated. Draw holes for the eyelet placement. Place the eyelets at the center of the piece for the best range of motion.

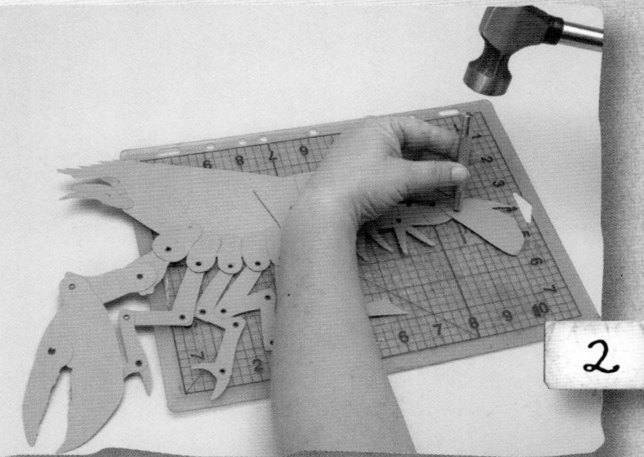

Assemble project

Use an eyelet tool and hammer to create holes for all the eyelets. Place 2 adjoining pieces together, overlapping the eyelet holes. Place an eyelet through both holes and use an eyelet tool and hammer to attach the eyelet. If the eyelets will show, be sure that all the eyelet backs are on the back of the project.

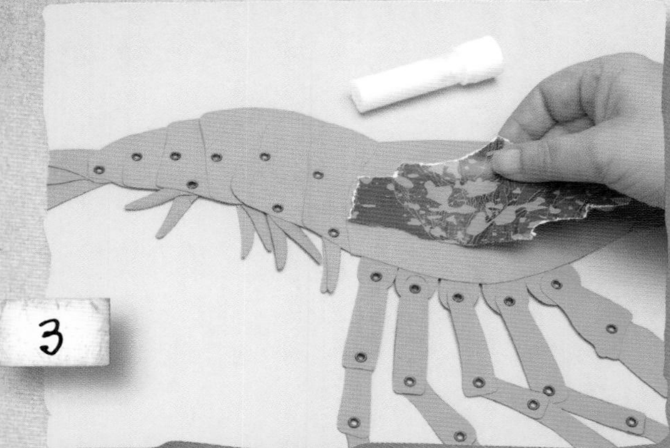

Collage to cover eyelets

Use a glue stick to adhere torn bits of images over the selected areas of the subject, including the eyelets. Be sure the collaged pieces do not overlap any joints, or you won't be able to move the pieces.

Paint project

Use oil paint sticks or any other medium to cover your subject, including the collaged pieces. Embellish as desired. I cut elastic cord for tentacles and fibers for antennae.

Attach to background

Create a background for your subject, if you don't already have one in mind. Cut a circle approximately 2" (5cm) in diameter. Place the background on a cutting mat and place the circle where you would like to attach your subject. Use an eyelet tool and hammer to put a hole in the center of the circle and the background paper. Place the eyelet in the hole and flip the background paper over. Use the eyelet tool and hammer to spread the back of the eyelet to secure. Use a glue stick to adhere the lobster to the circle. This method allows the entire object to pivot.

Dive into Life
Hope M. Clinchot

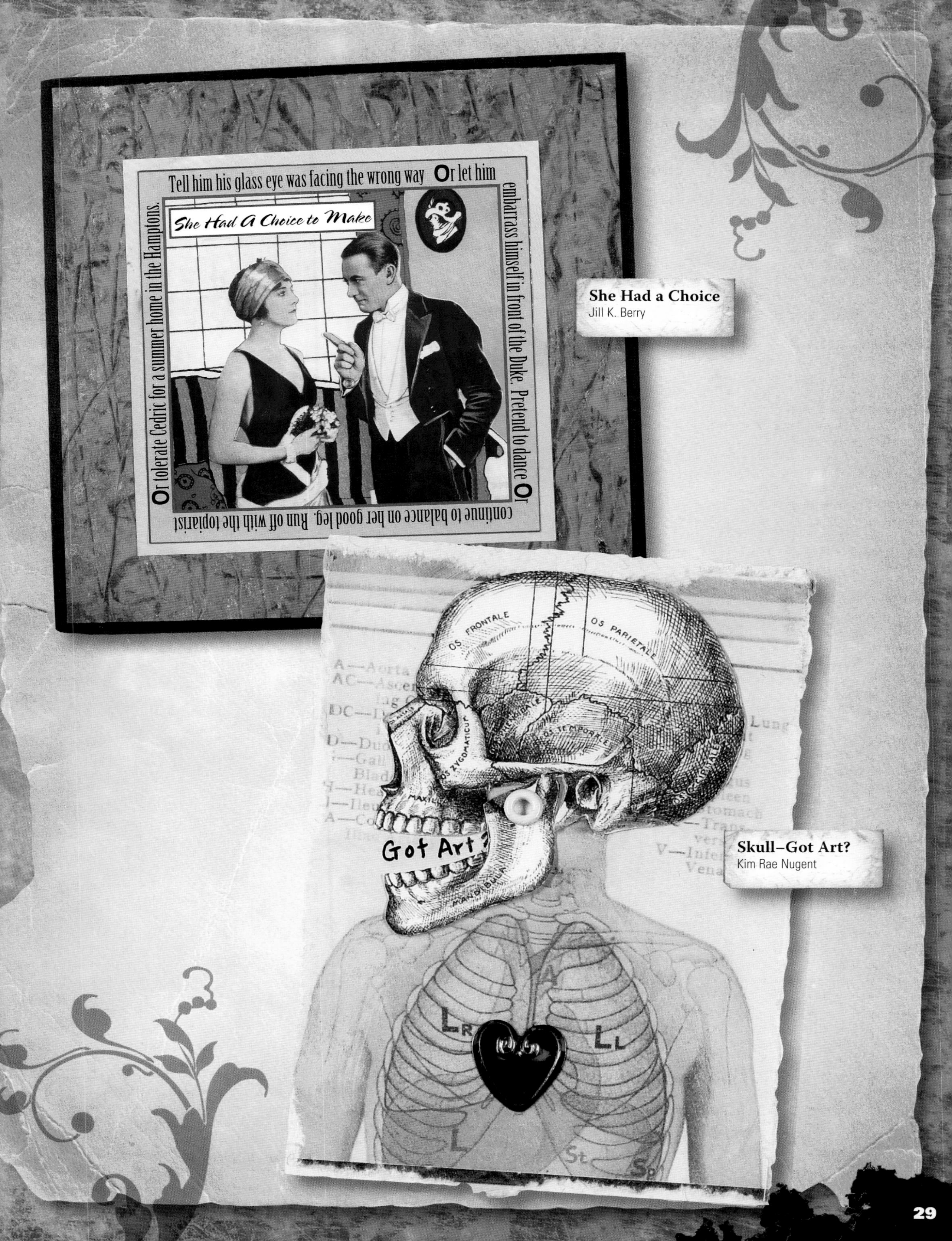

She Had a Choice
Jill K. Berry

Skull–Got Art?
Kim Rae Nugent

Wish upon a Star

Chapter 2
Artful Enigmas

Use maze, slide and magnetic puzzles to turn your work into playful pieces of interactive art that are anything but child's play. In this chapter, you'll learn how to add action to your art by incorporating puzzles with built-in motion. Start by using a simple maze puzzle as an accent or as the subject of the art (page 32). You can then move on to slicing and dicing an image or piece of art and attaching it to a slide puzzle (page 36). Solving the slide puzzle to reveal the artwork adds instant amusement to any piece. If you're going for something a little more artistic and are ready to step up your game, you can use magnets and metal pieces to create your own *Magnetic Personality* (page 40).

Wish upon a Star

Maze Puzzle

Recycling a plastic maze puzzle is an easy way to add an interactive element to your art. The nature of this type of puzzle lends itself to themes of movement, change and journeys. These puzzles can be found in a variety of shapes to fit your theme. This is a great way to feature children's artwork or images of family and friends. To illustrate this technique, I chose a star-shaped puzzle. For *Wish upon a Star*, I copied a picture of my Grandmother Eleanore and showcased her wistful expression in a way no plain photograph could. Included with the maze puzzle is a simple watercolor background technique using salt.

Materials

- cardstock
- heavyweight watercolor paper
- plastic maze puzzle
- scissors
- craft knife
- cutting mat
- water-based dimensional adhesive
- glue stick
- eyelets
- eyelet tool set and hammer
- pencil

optional materials

- photo
- black and silver permanent markers
- self-adhesive gemstones
- ribbon
- coarse salt
- acrylic paint
- mop paintbrush 1" (3cm)

1

Paint background

Use a piece of watercolor paper slightly larger than the size of your finished piece will be. Paint your background any way you choose. To achieve the look shown here, use a 1" (3cm) mop paintbrush to brush water over the entire surface of the watercolor paper. Paint a wash of acrylic paint on the wet paper. I used Phthalo Blue and Burnt Umber.

2

Add texture to background

Create a textured background that enchances the theme of your interactive element. For the look shown here, sprinkle coarse salt over the paper. Paint will pool around the salt to give the illusion of stars. Weigh down the edges of the watercolor paper so it dries flat. Let it dry and then brush off the salt.

Safety Tip

Use care when removing the maze's back. Point the craft knife away from you to avoid injury. Use slight pressure to prevent breaking the puzzle backing or blade.

3

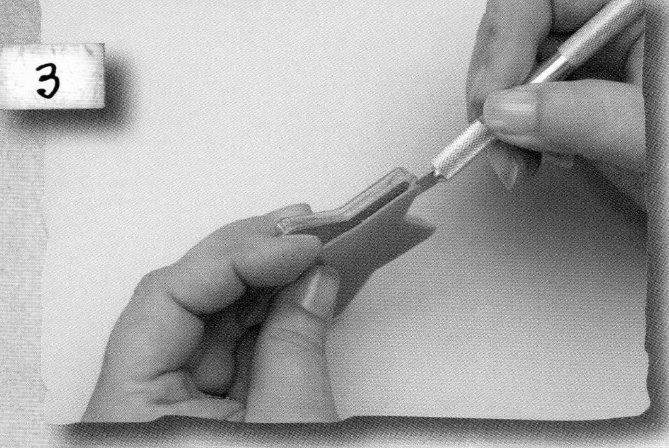

Prepare puzzle

Flip the puzzle over and look for a loose place where the backing meets the puzzle cover. Insert a craft knife between the backing and cover of the puzzle. Go around the entire edge using a slight twisting motion to remove the backing. Save the paper insert to use as a template in step 4. Set the ball and backing aside to use in step 5.

4

Cut out background and star

Find a section of paper that appeals to you and cut out a background for your work [in this case, a 3¾" × 5½" (10cm × 14cm) rectangle]. This is the background. Choose a lighter section of paper to trace and cut out a new background for your puzzle.

5

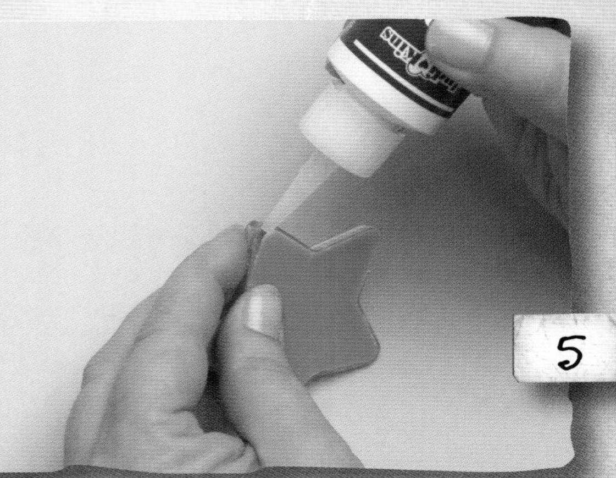

Attach puzzle

Place the ball back in the maze. Place the new puzzle background over the back and adhere the backing to the puzzle with water-based dimensional adhesive.

6

Attach background

Cut a rectangle that is slightly larger than your background from cardstock in the color of your choice. Attach the background to the cardstock with 4 silver metal eyelets. Adhere the puzzle to the background with water-based dimensional adhesive.

7

Embellish

Embellish your piece any way you choose. I attached the photo with a glue stick, then added self-adhesive gemstones and ribbon. I then wrote "Wish upon a Star" with permanent black and silver markers.

Starry Eyed
Lou McCulloch

Mind Games
Kim Rae Nugent

Round and Round
Joan E. Hollnagel

Pieces of Me Journal

Slide Puzzle

The shape-shifting workings of a slide puzzle provide you with an interesting way to alter your work. Dividing art into a moveable grid is a great way to explore different composition possibilities. You can also incorporate the frame of the puzzle into your design. This would be a fun addition to any card or gift topper—send it jumbled and let the recipient solve the puzzle to reveal a birthday greeting or cherished photo.

Frida Kahlo's practice of using her own image to explore artistic ideas was my impetus for using a picture of myself. Painting pink highlights on my photo was a fun way to experiment with new hairdos, or should I say hair don'ts. Try painting on a copy of a picture to add your own artistic flair.

Expand your art

Use the background underneath the puzzle as another canvas. Sections will be revealed one by one as you move the puzzle pieces around.

Materials

- image
- slide puzzle
- transparency
- paper trimmer
- scissors
- water-based dimensional adhesive
- straightedge
- pencil
- permanent marker

optional materials

- alphabet stamps
- journal
- acrylic paint
- craft knife
- cutting mat
- E-6000
- matte gel medium

1

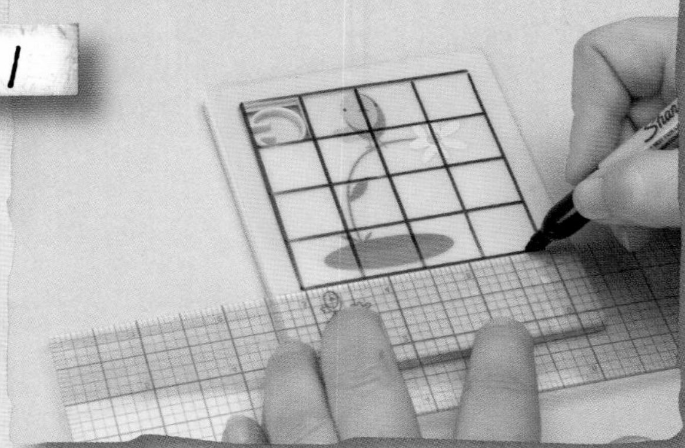

Create template

Place the transparency over the slide puzzle. Use a permanent marker and a straightedge to mark the grid lines of the puzzle onto the transparency. Cut the transparency to fit the grid template or around the slide puzzle frame if you want to incorporate it into your design.

2

Prepare photo

Center the template over the photo and trace around the edges. Cut the photo to size. I cut mine to cover the entrie slide puzzle. Embellish the photo with acrylic paint, if desired. I used light orange and hot pink to add highlights and to cover the background.

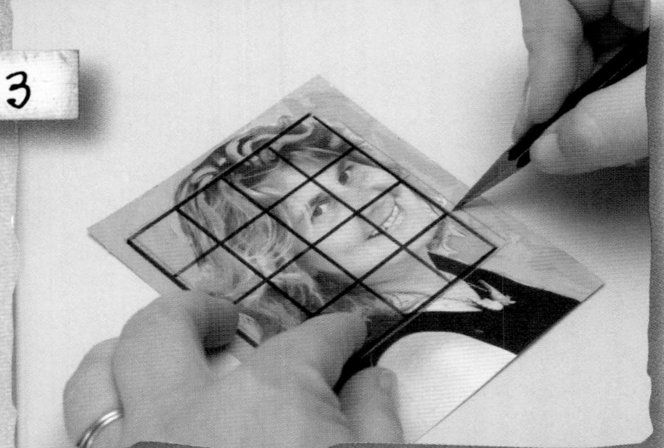

Mark photo

If your photo covers the entire slide puzzle, lay the grid template minus the frame over the picture again to determine the best placement. Use a pencil to trace the template onto the photo. Move the template down ¼" (6mm) to mark vertical grid lines along the top. Realign the template with the top line, then move the template in ¼" (6mm) from 1 of the side lines and mark the horizontal grid lines. Remove the template and extend the grid lines with a pencil and a straightedge.

Cut photo into squares

Use a paper trimmer or a craft knife to trim along the grid lines. (When using a paper trimmer, line the arrows on the trim blade with the outside line of the grid of the photo.)

Adhere pieces to puzzle

Lay the photo pieces onto the slide puzzle. Use scissors to trim any excess edges of each piece to make it fit and slide easily on the puzzle. Use water-based dimensional adhesive to adhere the backs of the photo pieces to the puzzle. If you set aside the frame in step 4, attach it to the puzzle case. Then embellish or add to the project of your choice. I then used alphabet stamps, matte gel medium and acrylic paint to embellish a journal. I then used E-6000 to adhere the puzzle to the journal cover.

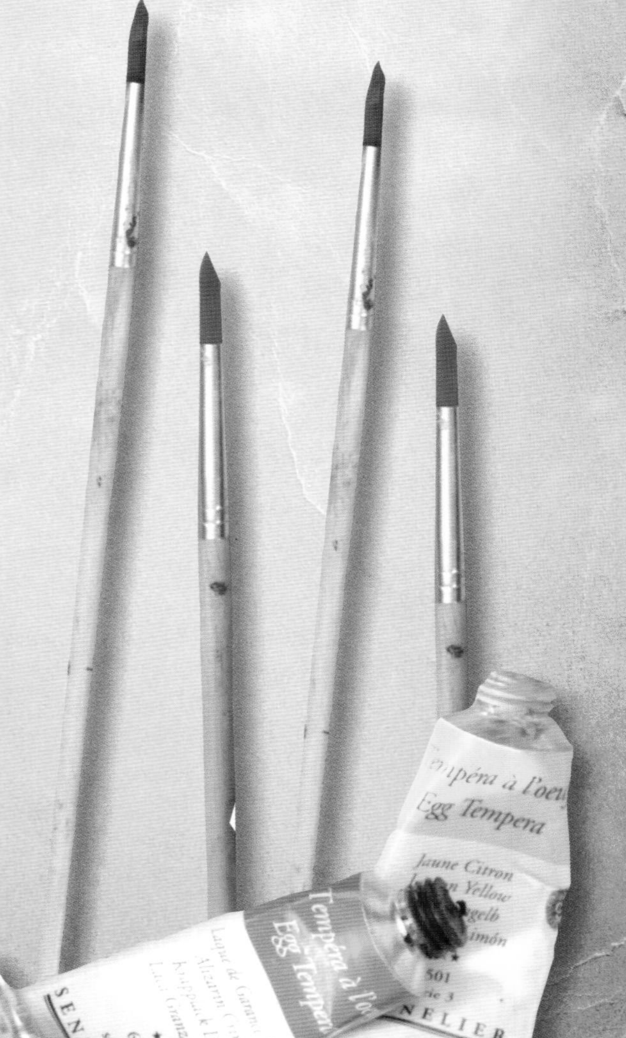

Basquiat Puzzles
Rita Bellanca

Go Fish
Deb Mortl

go fish

SEARCHING

for NIRVANA

Searching
Paula Strains

Expand your art
Attach your slide puzzle to a journal or a card for a one-of-a-kind piece of interactive art.

Magnetic Personality

Magnetic Puzzle

Remember the Wooly Willy? This fun childhood toy was the inspiration for this technique. Rearrange small metal pieces under plastic by waving a magnetic wand over them. Enhance your design with washers, staples, metal shavings or other small metal pieces. (I found the diamond shape of these points, used in framing pictures, an appealing choice for this technique.) You can choose to go as artistic or silly as you want with this versatile technique.

Materials

- mat board
- cardstock
- magnet
- metal tape
- small metal pieces
- ribbon
- rigid clear plastic sheet
- wood craft stick
- paper trimmer
- all-purpose glue
- spring clamps
- eyelet tool set and hammer
- straightedge
- pencil

optional materials

- colored pencils
- permanent marker
- craft knife
- cutting mat

1

Prepare image

Create your desired image. Try drawing or painting an original image, cutting an image from a magazine or using an old photo. I drew a simple figure on white cardstock then cut it into parts. Next, I traced around the pieces onto colored cardstock and colored it in with colored pencils. Save the cut pieces of cardstock for step 5, if desired.

Testing

Before assembling the piece, test to ensure that the magnet is strong enough to move your metal pieces.

2

Create frames

Cut 3 pieces of mat board, 6" × 8" (15cm × 20cm) each. Reserve 1 as the base piece and make frames from the remaining 2 pieces. Use a pencil and a straightedge to mark an opening for the frame—the opening should be slightly smaller than the imag you created or chose in step 1. Use a paper trimmer or a craft knife to cut the opening into the mat board.

3

Adhere drawing and frames

Use an all-purpose glue to adhere the focal image to the base piece. Then adhere 1 of the frames to the mat board backing. (Use care to make sure the edges are well attached to prevent the small metal parts you'll add later from becoming caught between the frame layers.) Place the metal points on the drawing. Cut rigid plastic to size, overlapping about ¼" (6mm) on all sides, and adhere with the all-purpose glue. Adhere the second frame over the plastic covering with the all-purpose glue. Use spring clamps to hold the sides together while the glue is drying.

Cover (optional)

Cover your frame however you'd like. For the look shown here: Cut 4 pieces of metal tape to fit the frame; leave enough tape to wrap around the frame's edges. Line the tape up with the inside edge of the frame at the top. Use your fingers to smooth the metal tape to remove any wrinkles or bubbles. Wrap the tape around the top edge. Repeat for the bottom edge. Then repeat for the sides.

Embellish frame (optional)

Embellish your fame any way you choose. I used a pencil or stylus to trace the outline of the figure from step 1 to create a pattern on the metal tape.

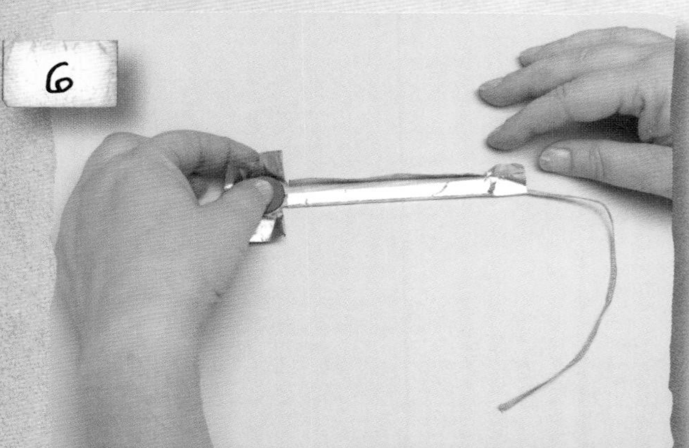

Create magnetic wand

Adhere a magnet to the tip of a wood craft stick with all-purpose glue. Cut the metal tape to the approximate size and shape of the wand. Lay the metal tape flat with the adhesive side up. Center the ribbon on the tape and run it along the length of the wood craft stick. Wrap the metal tape around the wood craft stick and the sides of the magnet. Trim the excess metal tape and embellish the wand, if desired.

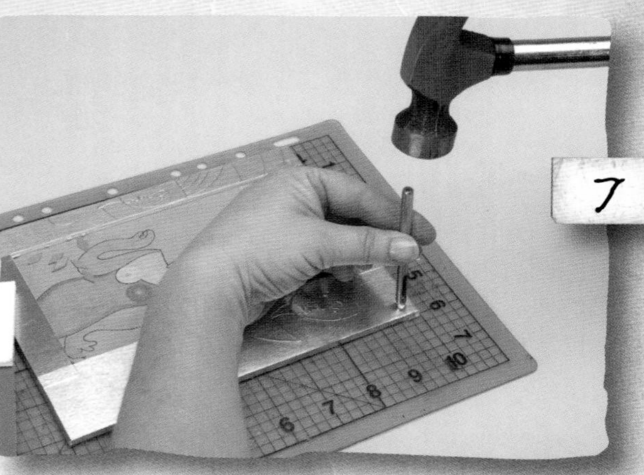

Attach wand

Use an eyelet tool and a hammer to make a hole through all the layers of the mat board. Tie the wand's ribbon to the frame.

Bearded Baroness
Jill K. Berry

Hairy Harriet

Is Harriet going out clean-shaven or au natural? You decide!

Hairy Harriet
Rita Bellanca

Stars
Gwynn Thoma

Chapter 3
Pull Tabs

You can accomplish an incredible amount of movement by adding a simple tab mechanism. You can also create moving tabs designed to reveal hidden art or messages. Start with a simple tab engineered to move a portion of your art piece. Facial expressions are great for this. I'll show you how to bring your faces to life with movable eyes and mouths (pages 50 and 54). Or move the tab to create a change of scenery (page 46) or to reveal a hidden message (page 58). And, you'll learn how to make guides and stops, so your artwork will never go off track.

A Bird Calls
From wing swept hair
the raven sprang.
The crow flies home
to reach the sun.
A bird calls
signs from you.
My heart flutters
spirits rise.
open my window
From wing swept hair
the raven sprang.
The crow flies home
to reach the sun.
A bird calls
signs from you.
My heart flutters
spirits rise.

Window Tab

Pull a tab to reveal a second image in a window opening. This is a fairly simple mechanism, and with the addition of guides and stop pieces you will be able to control the placement of your images with ease. If you want to send your interactive art as a postcard, as I did, see the tip on page 48 for size specifications. I am using a literal window to illustrate this technique, but you can apply it to anything that slides open to reveal another image.

When you are working, it sometimes helps to escape to a fresh environment. This project is made from a photo I took looking out the window of one of my favorite coffee shops, while waiting for my muse, the raven, to show. Consider taking a picture of one of your favorite haunts to use for this technique.

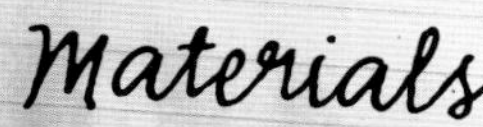

- image
- cardstock
- paper trimmer
- craft knife
- cutting mat
- glue stick
- 1" (3cm) circle punch

optional materials

- fine-point marker

1

Prepare background

Start with an image that allows you to slide a tab underneath to reveal a second image. I used a 4" × 6" (10cm × 15cm) photo of a double-hung window scene. Add text, if desired. I highlighted areas by outlining them with a fine-point marker.

2

Cut space for image tab

Cut a hole in the image where you want to reveal the second image. I cut out the lower half of the window with a sharp craft knife.

3

Cut guides and stop

Cut 2 guide pieces from cardstock (shown in orange) — these should be the same length as the project and a width that will fit between your cut shape from step 1 and the sides. Cut a stop piece from cardstock— this piece should fit between the guide pieces and be as wide as you want your pull-tab opening in step 5 to be. The guides and stop provide a track for the tab piece to slide up and down and prevent the tab from slipping from side to side. Use a glue stick to adhere the guide pieces and stop piece to the back of the picture.

Cut a tab

Measure the space between the guide pieces and the stop piece. Use a paper trimmer to cut a tab from the cardstock that fits those measurements.

Attach images

Place the tab behind the picture with the bottom of the tab touching the stop piece. Adhere the first image, which is the piece you removed in step 2 in the opening. Pull the tab up so the first image has completely disappeared. Then create or select a second image (here, I chose a bird) in the opening.

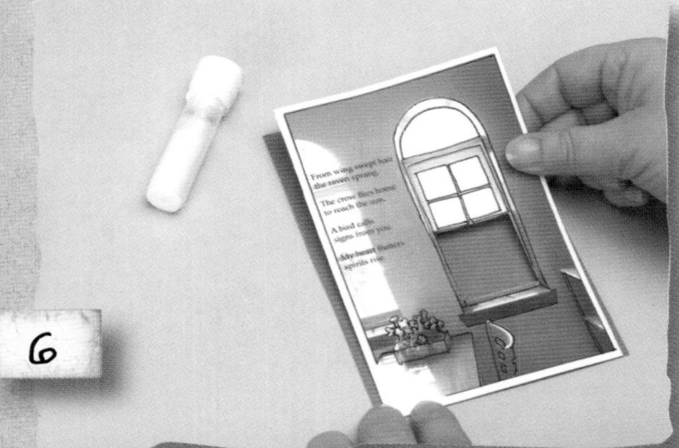

Attach backing

Cut a piece of cardstock to the size of the project for the backing. Put glue on the guide pieces, center the picture and adhere it to the backing.

Insert tab

Punch a half circle with a 1" (3cm) circle punch above the window opening. Slide the tab into place.

Save Money

If you want to make an interactive postcard, like I did here, design your card to fit within the United States Postal Service specification of 3½"–4¼" × 5"–6" (9cm–10cm × 13cm–15cm) to pay the postcard rate.

Decisions, Decisions
Cheryl Husmann

Blackbird Sings
Deb Mortl

Imagine
Hope M. Clinchot

An eye
for
art.
pull me

Shifting-Eye Tab

The eye tab is one of my favorite projects. Remember the old murder mystery movies in which a pair of moving eyes mysteriously appears in a portrait painting? Add a bit of mystery to your art with this modus operandi.

Moving the tab back and forth gives the illusion of shifty eyes. A face that has already been created can easily be copied and made interactive with this technique. Or, you can create a face specifically with this technique in mind.

Materials

- cardstock
- paper trimmer
- craft knife
- cutting mat
- glue stick
- pencil

1

Create holes for eyes

Choose an existing image of a face or create a new one. Place the piece face up on your work surface. Cut out eye openings using a sharp craft knife.

2

Apply guides and stop

Using a paper trimmer, cut a strip of cardstock wider than the eye openings and long enough to span the width of the project. Lay this strip, which will be the eye tab, so it covers the eye openings and extends past the side. Leave the strip in place to position the guides and stop pieces. Cut 2 more strips of cardstock that are the width of the project for guides. Cut 1 piece for a stop—it should fit between the guide pieces and be as wide as you want the pull tab to be. Use a glue stick to adhere the guide and stop pieces to the back of the picture around the eye tab. Leave enough slack to allow the eye tab to move freely.

Mark pupils

Place the eye tab in the slot until it stops. Mark the pupils in the eye opening. Remove the eye tab. Use a glue stick to adhere a picture of irises, or draw them.

Cover back

Attach a backing sheet that's the same size as your work; be sure to run the glue stick around the outside edge of the backing sheet, the guide and the stop pieces to create a pocket for the eye tab.

Lion and Native
Jill K. Berry

Soul of the Gypsy
Judy Wise

Gypsy Fatbook
Kim Rae Nugent

Mary's Magic Garden
Hope M. Clinchot

Speaks Her Mind

Mouth Tab

Not only has this piece been designed with a mouth that opens and closes, but it also does this task within set parameters made possible by guides and stops. This prevents the mouth from opening too far or closing too much, and it prevents missing lips. Try it without guides and a stop, and you will see what I mean.

While designing this piece, I remembered a small picture of a face I had clipped from a magazine. I was particularly attracted to the simple graphic image with strong lines and vivid colors. I created my own image reminiscent of that style. Not until I received contributing artist Rita Bellanca's *Basquiat Puzzles* (page 39), did I find out that the image that had inspired me was by the American artist Jean-Michel Basquiat.

- image
- backing paper
- cardstock
- materials to color or paint
- paper trimmer
- craft knife
- cutting mat
- glue stick

optional materials

- watercolor paper

Cut out mouth

Start with the image of a face with an open mouth. Cut out the lower lip and the inside of the mouth portion with a sharp craft knife. Leave the upper lip and teeth intact.

Create mouth mechanism

Use a glue stick to adhere the lower lip and mouth to a piece of watercolor paper or cardstock. Color or paint the background to match the face tone. The portion below the lip will act as the chin when the mouth is closed, so be sure that it matches the original image. Cut the mouth mechanism in the shape of a T, making sure the bottom fully covers the mouth space and extends past your project piece to create a tab pull.

Apply guides

Position the lower mouth piece so the mouth is fully open. Flip it over. Using a paper trimmer, cut 2 strips of cardstock to line up with the bottom of the project and extend to the bottom of the T and wide enough to fit betwen the side of the T and the side of the paper. Use a glue stick to adhere the guide pieces.

Apply stop

Keep the mouth tab within the guides from step 3. Push the lower mouth piece so the mouth is closed. Flip it over. Using a paper trimmer, cut a strip of cardstock that spans the width of the project. Use a glue stick to adhere the stop piece on top of the T.

Cover back

Attach a backing sheet that's the same size as the work; be sure to run adhesive around the outside edge of the backing sheet, the guide and the stop pieces to create a pocket for the mouth tab.

Talk to Me
Sandra McCutcheon Pape

Mermaid
Judy Wise

Brown-Eyed Girl
Judy Wise

pull my feather

Hold Fast to Dreams

Removable Quote

Because this tab is made from a part of the primary image, design it so it is fully incorporated into the art as part of the image. In this case, it is the tip of a feather Also, design it so that when you remove it completely, it stands as a piece of art on its own, perhaps revealing a quote. This works well for any layered, overlapping pieces: feathers, ruffles on a dress, petals and more.

Materials

- image—2 copies
- cardstock
- craft knife
- cutting mat
- glue stick
- writing utensil or printed quote

1

Create opening for quote

Select or create a subject you would like to articulate. For this project I repurposed an oil pastel drawing of mine. Make a copy. With a sharp craft knife, cut an opening in the space above where you want to insert the pull quote in image 1. Follow the contour of the shape (in this case, the feather).

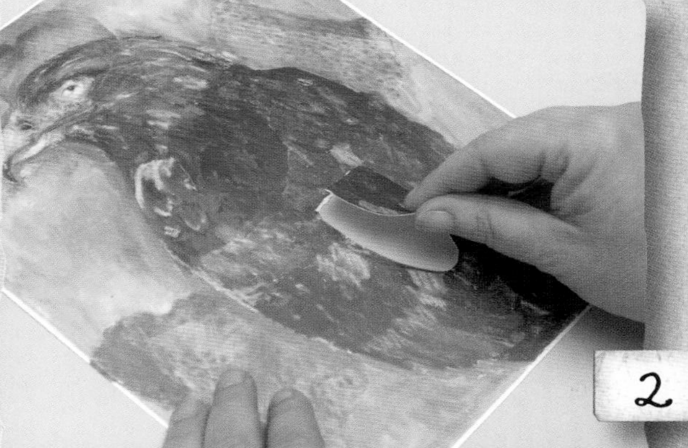

2

Cut out feather for quote

From image 2 cut the portion of the image you want to use as a pull. You can make a clean cut if you wish. Here, I hand-tore the edge to "feather" it.

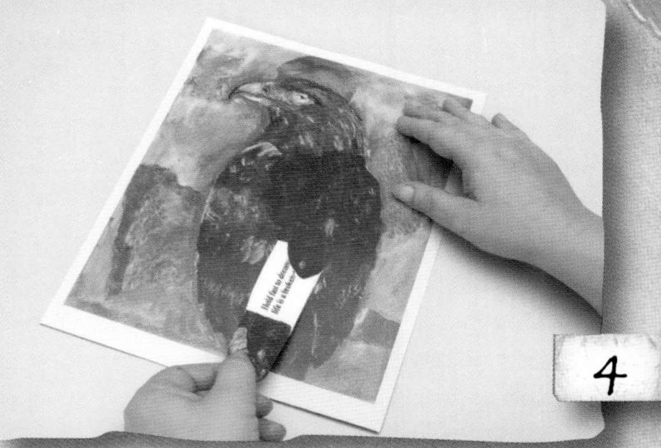

Create removable quote

Use a glue stick to adhere the cut-out image portion from step 2 to a piece of white cardstock. Hand write or adhere a printed quote alongside it in the space that will become the tab. Sketch in the outline of the tab so it is long enough to prevent it from becoming lost inside your artwork when pushed all the way in.

Insert quote and finish

Cut out the quote tab and place it into the opening cut in step 1. Use a glue stick to adhere a piece of cardstock the same size as the project to the back of the project piece.

Come out of your shell and discover life's possibilities.

Ethan Owl
Kim Rae Nugent

Turtle
Kim Rae Nugent

Chapter 4
Twists and Turns

Add some wow factor to your projects with the more complex tab mechanisms in this chapter. By combining a tab with a pivoting mechanism you can create intricate movement throughout your artwork. Start with the simple swing lever (page 74) for a hinge effect, perfect for a mouth you can open and close. Morphing one image into something completely unexpected by effortlessly sliding a tab evokes oohs and ahhs. There are multiple ways you can achieve this effect. Try both the revolving picture and behind bars tabs to see which one you prefer (pages 68 and 78). Move hinged doors, limbs and more with the flapping-door tab (page 64); and insert more surprises by adding artwork to the inside of the open door or hand. Master these intricate yet easy-to-make techniques, and add wonder to all of your pieces.

open me
ONE WAY
SPEED LIMIT 25
MILE-DIAL
COMPUTES YOUR GASOLINE MILEAGE
SET GALLONS OPPOSITE MILES
READ MILEAGE IN WINDOW
MINNESOTA
Duluth
OHIO

One-Way Lena

Flapping-Door Tab

Pull a tab and open a door to create an element of surprise. Adding artwork to the inside of the door adds even more interest to the finished piece. This technique is made for doors, but can be used to move any jointed object, such as elbows, knees and toes.

When creating interactive art, consider all the surfaces that will be visible and treat them with surface decoration. For *One-Way Lena*, I painted even the inside of the car door and I found a picture of my Great Aunt Lena in a sitting position. Painting over images is a simple way to solve design dilemmas without the need for a photo-editing program.

Materials

- 2 images—multiple copies of each
- heavyweight watercolor paper
- scissors
- craft knife
- cutting mat
- all-purpose glue
- glue stick
- clamps
- ruler
- pencil

optional materials

- white gesso
- paint kit
- embellishments: wooden stick, ribbon, magnet, compass
- eyelet
- eyelet tool set and hammer

1

Prepare background

Create a background that complements your theme. Here, I used all-purpose glue to adhere the map pieces to heavy paper. To tone down the map, I then dry brushed white gesso over it.

2

Prepare photo

Print 1 copy of the photo that contains a door and 2 copies of the photo of what you want to be inside. Paint the 2 so that they will fit together naturally in your finished piece. I painted an iron metallic surfacer over the door to cover the figure in the photo and then painted the rest of the car. I then painted a second coat over the entire car. I then covered parts of the car with a rust antiquing solution. (When using antiquing solutions, follow the manufacturer's directions and safety precautions.)

3

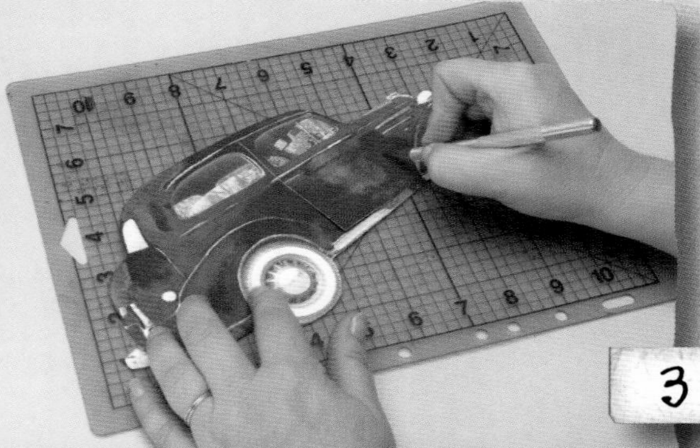

Remove door and adhere car

Use a craft knife to cut out the door. Set it aside for later. Adhere the image to the background panel from step 1.

Exposed

Movable art exposes several surfaces, so remember to decorate the back as well.

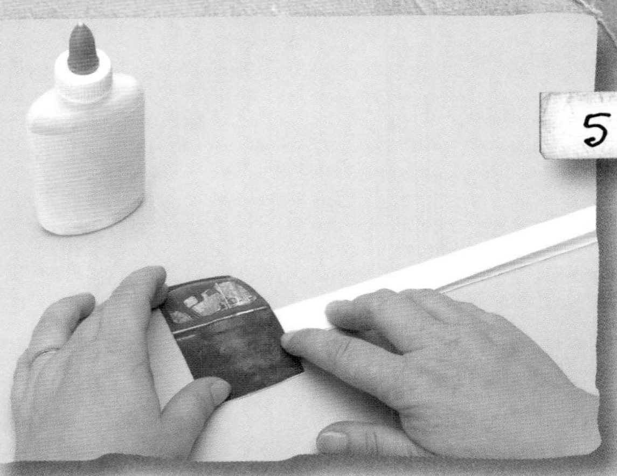

Create back of door

Trace the shape of the door cut out in step 3 onto heavyweight watercolor paper. Use scissors to cut out the new door. Paint it to match your painted subject from step 2.

Create pull strip

Measure the distance between the door and the side of the paper. Then cut a strip from heavyweight paper to the length you just measured plus an extra 1"–2" (3cm–5cm) to attach the pull tab. Fold the strip in half lengthwise and adhere the 2 sides together—this makes the strip more durable. Use all-purpose glue to adhere the door at the end of the strip. Flip the strip over and use all-purpose glue to attach the door you set aside in step 2 to the back of the first door, creating a double-sided door. Use clamps to hold the strip together as the glue dries.

Insert strip

Place the door on top of the image. Use a pencil to lightly mark the edges of the strip along the edges of the door. Use a craft knife to connect the 2 marks with a slit. Test to make sure the slit is wide enough to insert the strip. Insert the strip.

Attach cross piece

Flip the project over to the back. Fold the strip 180 degrees so it lays flat against the project and is now facing opposite the direction that it was on the front. Cut a cross piece from heavyweight paper that is longer than the movable object and about 1½" (4cm) wide. The cross piece helps to push the door shut. Fold the cross piece in half lengthwise and use all-purpose glue to adhere its sides together. Use all-purpose glue to adhere the cross piece to the underside of the strip.

Finish pull and embellish

Mark the edges of the strip at the back edge of the project. Use a craft knife to connect them with a slit. Insert the strip through the slit.

Create pull tab and embellish

Cut an image that goes with the theme of the project to serve as your pull tab. Trace the shape of the image onto heavyweight paper. Cut out the shape. Apply all-purpose glue to the backs of each piece and sandwich the strip between the 2 pieces. Embellish the background paper with images that reinforce the theme. I used copies of photos and a compass. Use all-purpose glue to attach the figure inside the door opening.

Hope Springs Eternal
Laurie Mika

Girl Blows Kisses
Kim Rae Nugent

There Is a Place

Revolving-Picture Tab

Move a lever to turn the wheel and transform one image into another. This technique is one of the most complex mechanisms in this book, but its wow factor makes it worth the effort. No need to design this mechanism yourself, I've included templates (page 118) for you to follow. The intricacy of this design is best handled with a technique that won't warp the paper, so I chose pen and ink to draw directly on the interactive parts. But you could also, choose to paint your image and make color photocopies of it. Then it's easy to print the templates directly onto your copied images.

Materials

- heavy cardstock in 2 colors
- backing paper
- craft knife
- cutting mat
- all-purpose glue

optional materials

- pen

practice makes perfect

I recommend making a practice piece first using two different colors of cardstock. After you are familiar with how this mechanism works, try using it in an art project.

Copy and cut pattern

Copy template 1 (page 118) onto 1 color of heavy cardstock. Copy template 2 (page 118) and the circle onto a different color of cardstock. Carefully cut the lines with a sharp craft knife. Accuracy is important for the mechanism to work properly. When you're finished cutting template 1, you'll have 6 tabs; leave this connected to the cardstock. Save the circle for later.

Connect templates

Lay template 1 over template 2. Slide tab 1 from template 1 under slit 1 on template 2. Repeat for tabs 2–6. Insert the arrow tab into the cut for the slide.

3

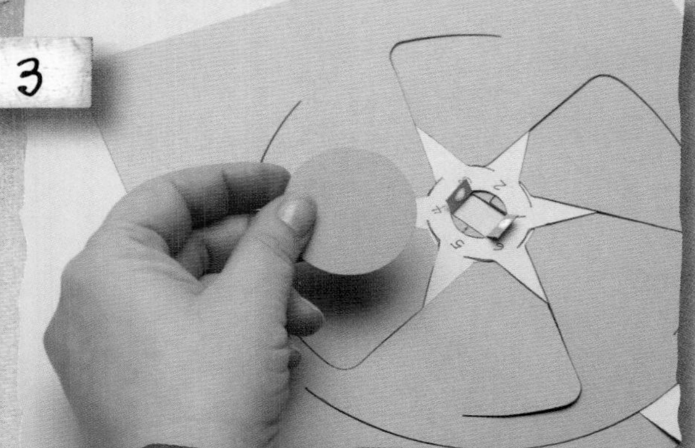

Test tab placement and cover

Fold tabs 3 and 6 over the circle opening in template 2. Hold the folded tabs down and slide the arrow tab to test the mechanism. The circle should change from one color to the next. If the mechanism becomes hung up, check to see that the cuts are made deep enough where the templates meet. Apply all-purpose glue to the folded tabs (not the circle) to adhere the circle from template 2 to the folded tabs.

4

Draw first image

Turn the tab so only the cardstock for template 1 is showing. Draw a picture onto template 1.

5

Draw second image

Turn the tab wheel to reveal the cardstock for template 2. Draw a second image.

This is the back view that shows what the revolving wheel looks like before the backing is applied.

Boundaries are important

Be sure to keep the portion of the drawing that you want to change within the confines of the flaps. The outer edge of the template won't change, so place anything here that you want for both images. I placed the quote on the outer edge so it would apply to both images.

Please Use Other Door

Heartfelt Man
Paula Strains

Heart Wide Open

see my heart

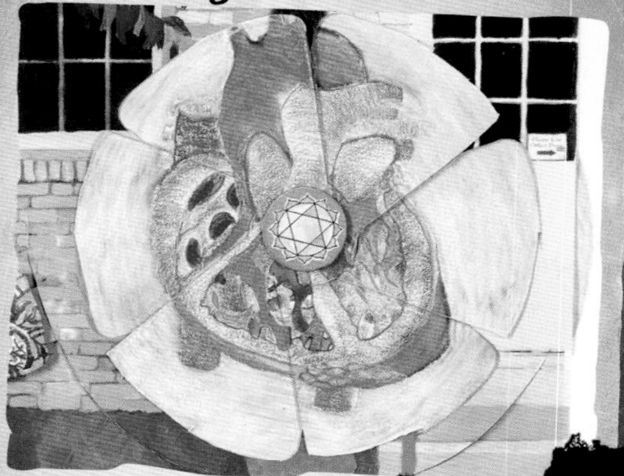

Hermit Crab
Kim Rae Nugent

Find a home that fits you.

A Crow by day

and Owl by night.

The soulful bird

doth take flight

A Crow by Day
Kim Rae Nugent

find the crab

Different backgrounds – Headed in opposite directions

Yet connected – They were Women

RAEVN '0

They Were Women
Kim Rae Nugent

change my direction

Little Fish

Swing-Lever Tab

The interactive mechanism for this technique allows the object to be moved with the use of a lever rather than by touching the object itself. It adds an element of surprise to see what moves when a lever is swung back and forth. As an added feature an object can be revealed when a section of art is moved.

- heavy cardstock
- paper trimmer
- scissors
- craft knife
- cutting mat
- all-purpose glue
- brad
- eyelet tool set and hammer
- pencil

1

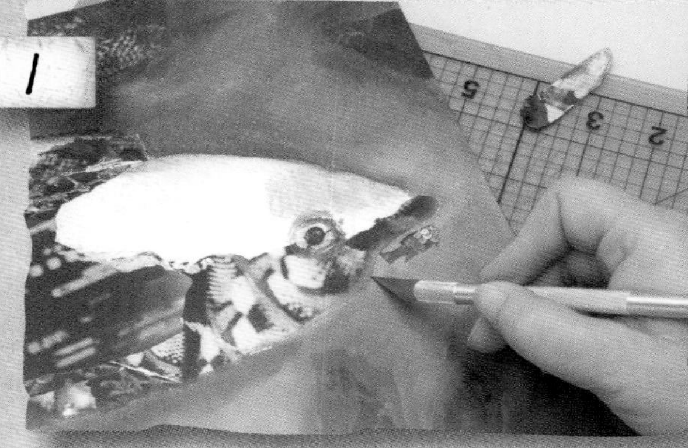

Prepare image

Draw, paint, copy or print the image you want to use for the project onto heavy cardstock. Then create the movable piece for the project on a separate piece of cardstock (here, I created the lower jaw of the subject's mouth). Use a craft knife to cut a slot on the project piece where you want to place the movable piece.

2

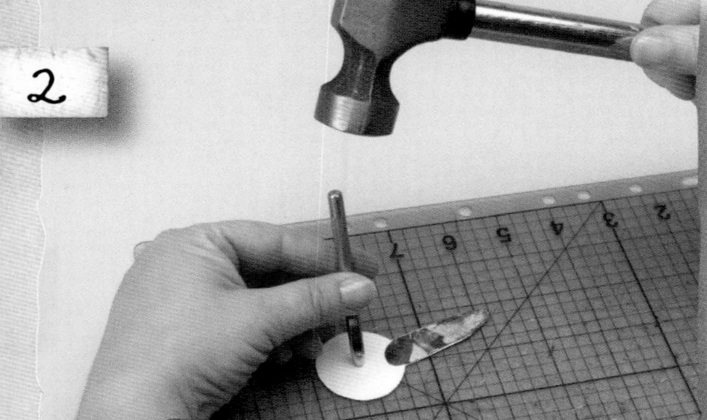

Create mechanism

Draw a circle that's proportionate to your movable piece onto heavy cardstock. The range of motion is directly proportional to the size of the circle—to increase the range of motion, draw a larger circle. Place your movable piece next to the circle, overlapping it slightly. Trace around the movable piece. Cut out the circle and movable piece from the cardstock. Use all-purpose glue to adhere the movable piece to the mechanism. Use an eyelet tool and hammer to place a hole in the center of the circle.

3

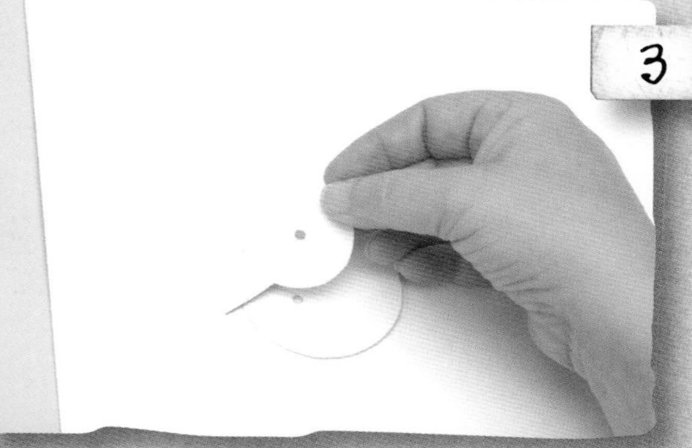

Create hole for pivot

Trace a circle that's larger than the circle from step 2 onto heavyweight paper. Use scissors to cut it out. Line up the larger circle with the edge of the slit you made in step 1. Insert the movable piece from step 2 into the slit on top of the larger circle. Use a pencil to mark the hole for the pivot point. Remove the large circle and use an eyelet tool and hammer to create a hole where you marked.

4

Attach circle

Place the brad through the back of the large circle. Apply all-purpose glue to the same side as the brad head and adhere the circle to the wrong side of the project piece adjacent to the slit. Insert the movable piece (lower jaw) through the slit and over the brad. Fold the brad prongs over the smaller circle.

5

Create lever

Use a paper trimmer to cut a strip of heavyweight paper—it needs to be long enough to stick out the side of the project when it's attached to the center of the moving mechanism. It should also be wide enough to fold in half lengthwise. Fold it lengthwise and use all-purpose glue to adhere the strip's halves together. Then use all-purpose glue to attach 1 end of the strip to the top circle of the moving mechanism.

Tip

You may want to test the mechanism before adhering the larger circle.

Who'll be the Clerk?

I, said the Lark,

If it's not in the dark,

I'll be the Clerk.

This is the Lark,

Saying "Amen" like a clerk.

Who Killed Cock Robin?
Joan E. Hollnagel

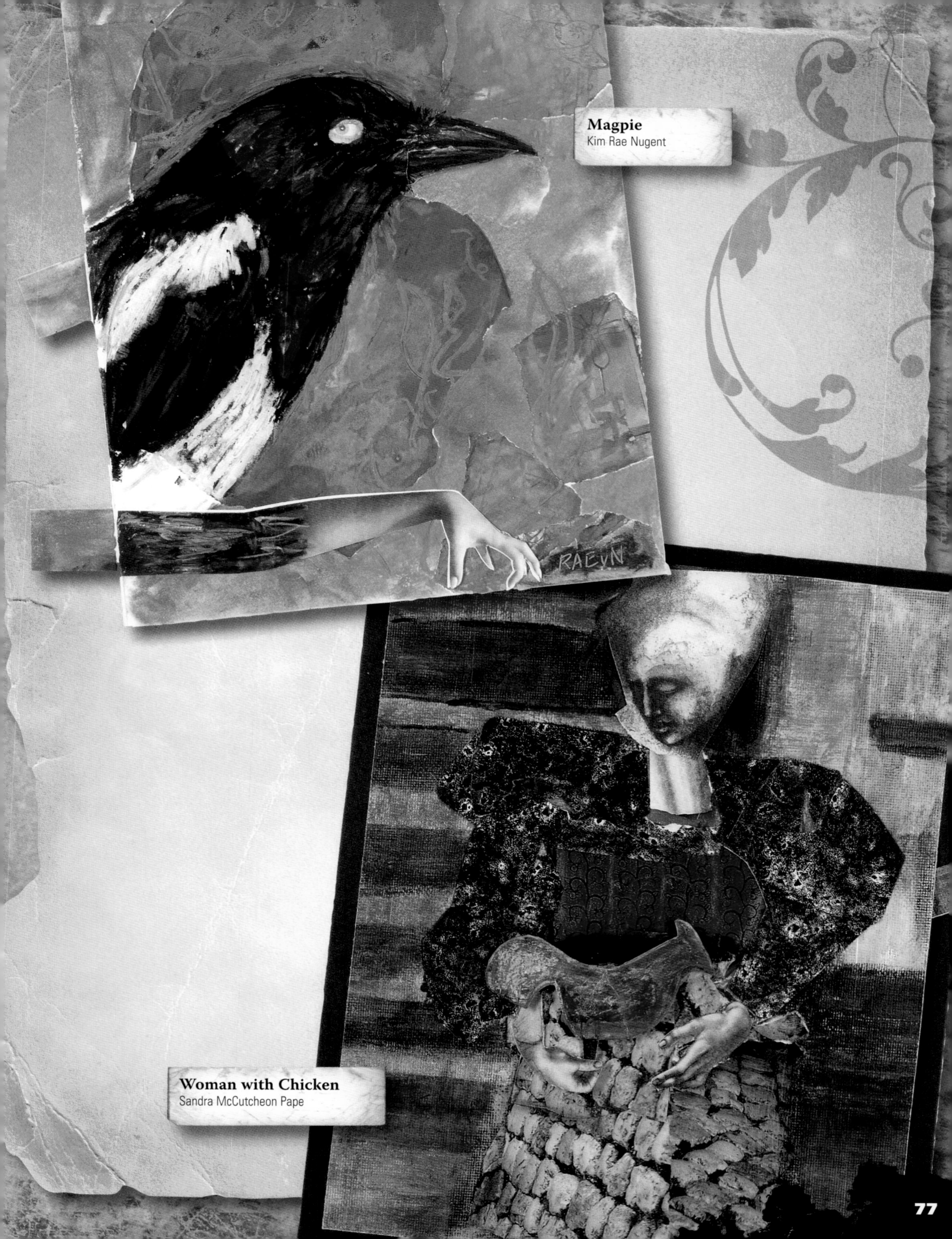

Magpie
Kim Rae Nugent

Woman with Chicken
Sandra McCutcheon Pape

Roar of the Lion

Le Cirque

see me roar

Behind-Bars Tab

This technique involves alternating bars and openings to showcase two different images, depending on which way the tab is pulled. To work effectively, the space between the bars must be equal to or slightly smaller than the bars. This technique can be approached two different ways: by drawing a continuous image between the bars or by cutting existing pictures into strips and combining them. The techniques are different, but the results are the same.

Materials

- heavyweight paper
- craft knife
- cutting mat

optional materials

- 1" (3cm) circle punch
- eyelets
- eyelet tool set and hammer

Drawing between bars

This technique employs two different images drawn together on one page. To accomplish this technique, you'll draw your first image between the bars, then move the tab and draw the second image. Note that sometimes it may be necessary to fudge the anatomy in order for important parts to be shown, making your object more recognizable. For example, I stretched the lion's body on the side view so his rear leg and tail would be visible. I've provided templates for the bars and the background (page 119) for you to easily add this technique to your interactive repertoire.

The finished movable piece

1

Remove bars

Copy the template (page 119) or create your own pattern. If you are making your own pattern, it is important to either make the bars and spaces the same width, or to make the spaces between the bars slightly smaller than the bars. Use a craft knife to remove the space between the bars and the slits for the pull tabs. Use a craft knife to remove any extra paper surrounding the template.

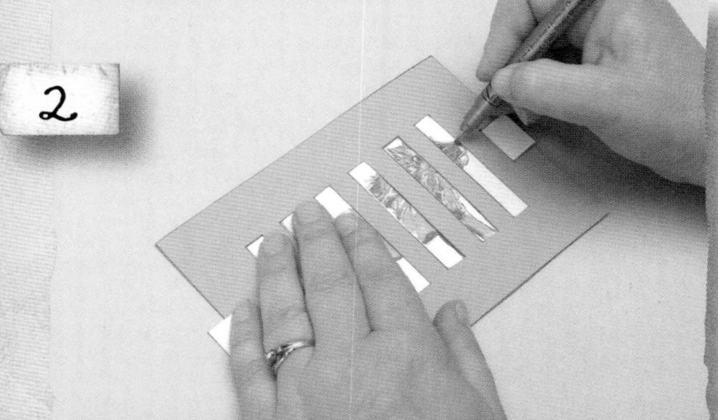

2

Draw first image

Cut out template 2 and insert the tabs into the slits. Push or pull the movable piece all the way to one side. Draw the first image through the bars.

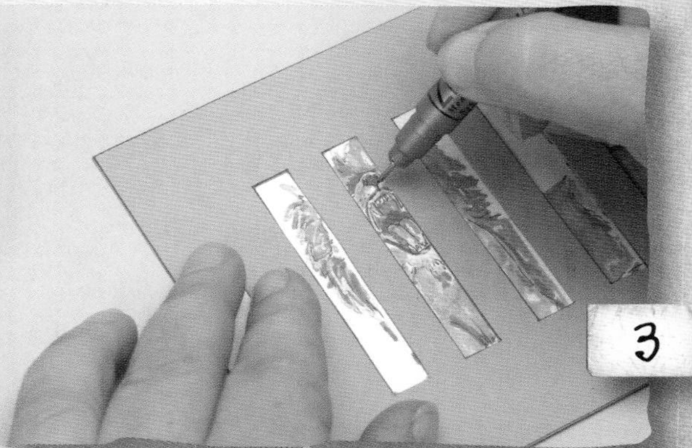

3

Draw second image and embellish

Push or pull the movable piece all the way to the opposite side. Draw the second image through the bars. Paint, collage or draw on the outside frame to convey the project's theme. I used eyelets to add wheels to create a circus wagon.

Art between bars

This technique requires two different images made separately. The width of the bars and spaces between them should be designed to showcase the most important features of your images. Because of their narrow width, I found it easier to cut the bars with my paper trimmer, rather than a craft knife.

My daughter Brook is the model for this project. For the second image I used oil pastels to color a mourning dove over a copy of her picture. Consider using two variations of one image for this technique.

Materials

- 2 images
- cardstock
- paper trimmer or craft knife
- glue stick
- pencil

pull me

Set Her Soul Free

1

2

Cut images

Copy the template (page 119) or create your own. Place template 1 over the first image, arranging it so the most important details are showing through the bars. For me it was the subject's eyes. Use a pencil to mark the bars onto the image. Use a paper trimmer or craft knife to cut the image into the strips you just marked. Repeat this process for the second image.

Alternate image strips

Lay out alternating strips of the 2 cut images (the first strip from image 1, the second strip from image 2, the third strip from image 1 and so on) side by side. Use a glue stick to adhere all the strips onto a piece of cardstock. If you're not using the templates, apply guides and stops to the back of the paper with the bars. (See the Window-Tab technique for instructions on guides and stops, page 46.)

Nebraska
Jill K. Berry

Why Crawl When You Can Soar ?
Cris Peacock

Duck to Water
Jan Drees

Journey
Lou McCulloch

Flower Garden
Paula Strains

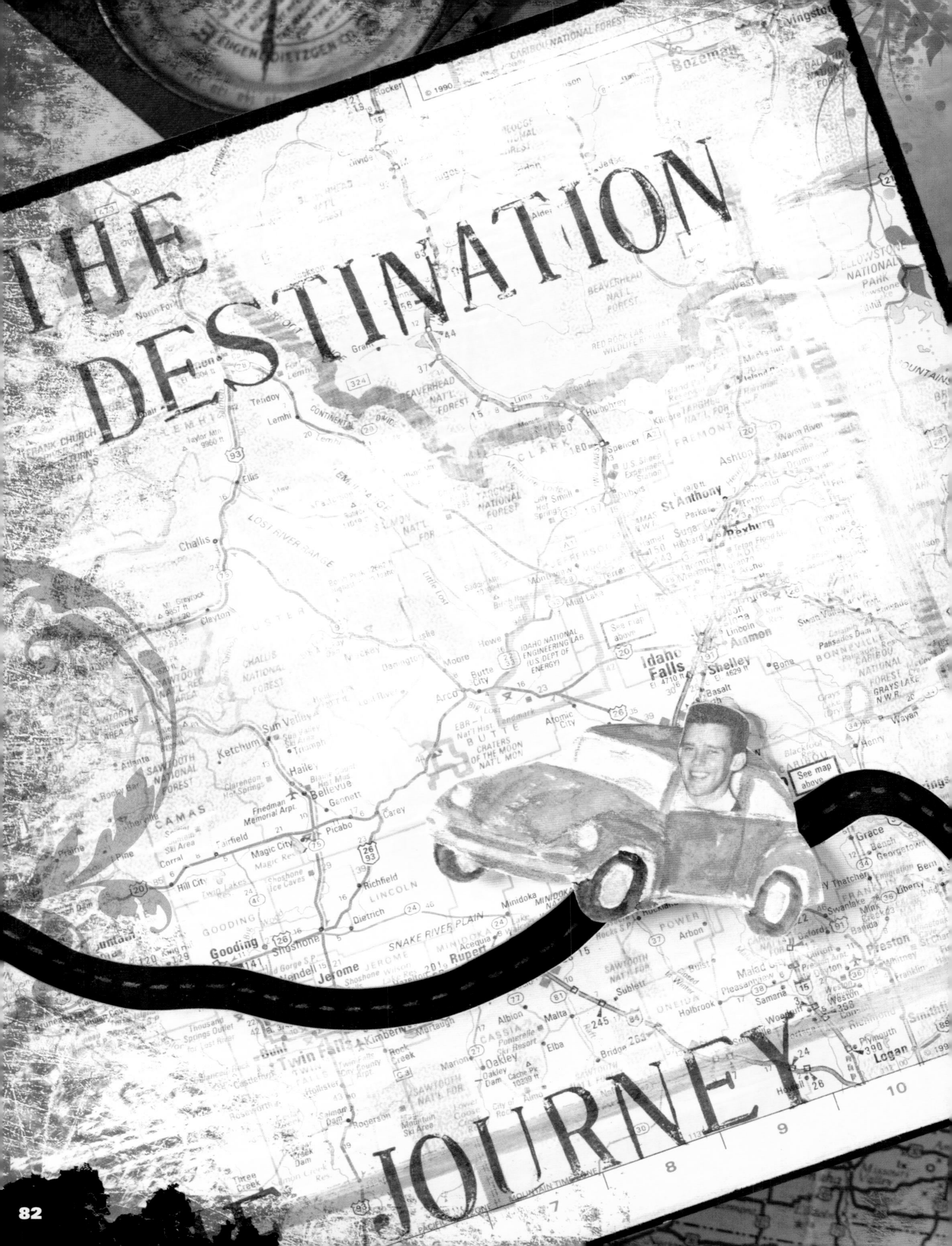
THE DESTINATION
JOURNEY

Chapter 5 Everything Else

Flaps, flips, slides and more—the mechanisms in this chapter are unique and fun to make.

Flaps are among the simplest interactive elements to include, but they add so much depth to a piece with their hidden messages and images. The image slide (page 94) is perfectly suited for art that reflects a journey—whether one of personal growth or an actual road trip. The hook-and-line mechanism enables you to make a graspable, touchable project (page 90).

Although the senses of sight and touch are the most common senses activated by art, don't forget smell and hearing. A simple recipe puts the sniff in scratch-and-sniff (page 106). Lastly, don't underestimate the fun of squeaky art even adults will enjoy (page 102). With these varied techniques you can learn to create stimulating art on many levels.

reveal my message
To be
enlightened
is to be
intimate
with
all things

Flipping Flap

Use a flap when you want to move a piece of your art to reveal an image or quote. As simple as flipping a switch, this technique enhances any artwork by adding an additional layer of texture. Open cabinet doors, jackets, wings and more to uncover messages or images that add visual interest or just some fun to your projects.

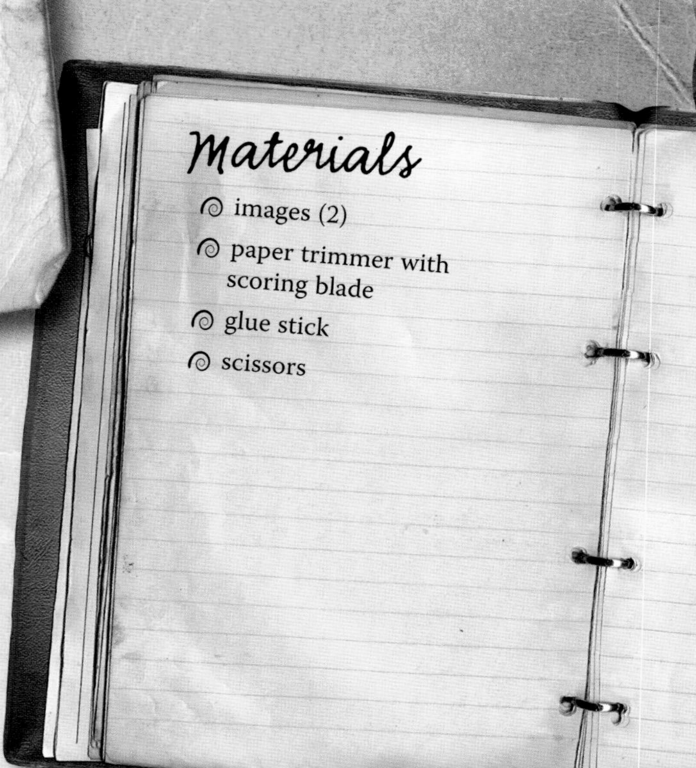

Incorporated art

This technique involves a smaller flap mounted onto a larger page. When the flap is turned it reveals another image that also incorporates the larger image. Use this technique when it's important to keep the continuity of the piece regardless of the flap's position. Flora, fauna or flourishes are some of the creative designs that lend themselves to this technique.

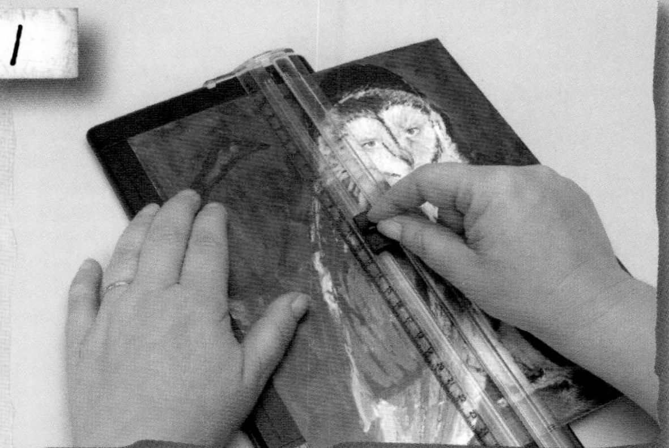

Score fold

Using the primary image, decide where you want your flap to fold. Use your paper trimmer with the scoring blade to score the entire length of the image.

Cut image

Start your cut at the top of the page and cut along the score line until you reach the image. Continue to cut, following the outline of the image.

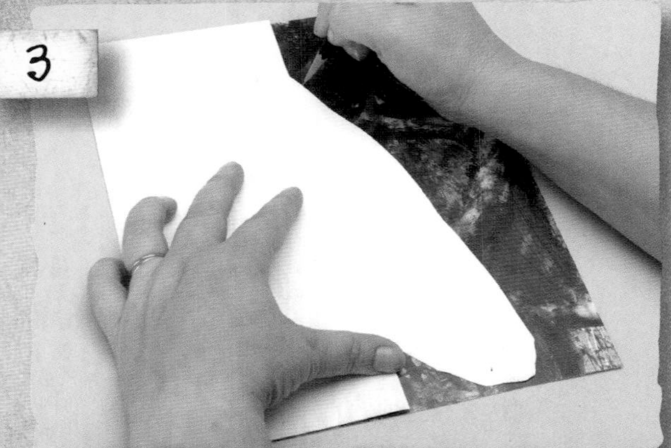

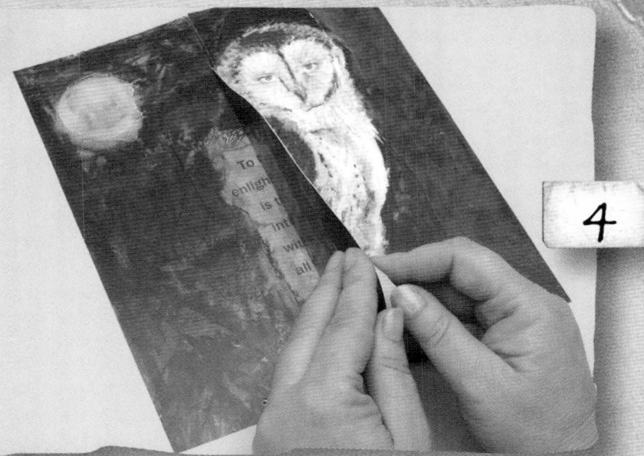

Create underside of flap

Place the primary scored image from step 2 facedown on a secondary image and lightly mark score lines from the primary image. Use a paper trimmer with scoring blade and score the secondary image. Replace the piece from step 2 facedown on this sheet, aligning the score lines. Extend the flap and trace around it. Cut the secondary image, following the score lines and the outline of the flap.

Attach flap

Turn the first image so it is facing up. Match the fold lines, with the flap's backs together. Use a glue stick to adhere the flap's undersides together.

School Days
Gina Louthian-Stanley

Old Woman with Dove
Sandra McCutcheon Pape

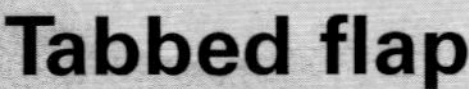

Tabbed flap

This technique is easier to execute and more straightforward than the flipping flap with incorporated art (page 85). Instead of being part of the image, the tab is simply inserted into a slit, allowing the flap to open and close. Because you won't see it, you don't have to embellish the tab.

Materials

- image
- heavyweight paper
- craft knife
- cutting mat
- all-purpose glue

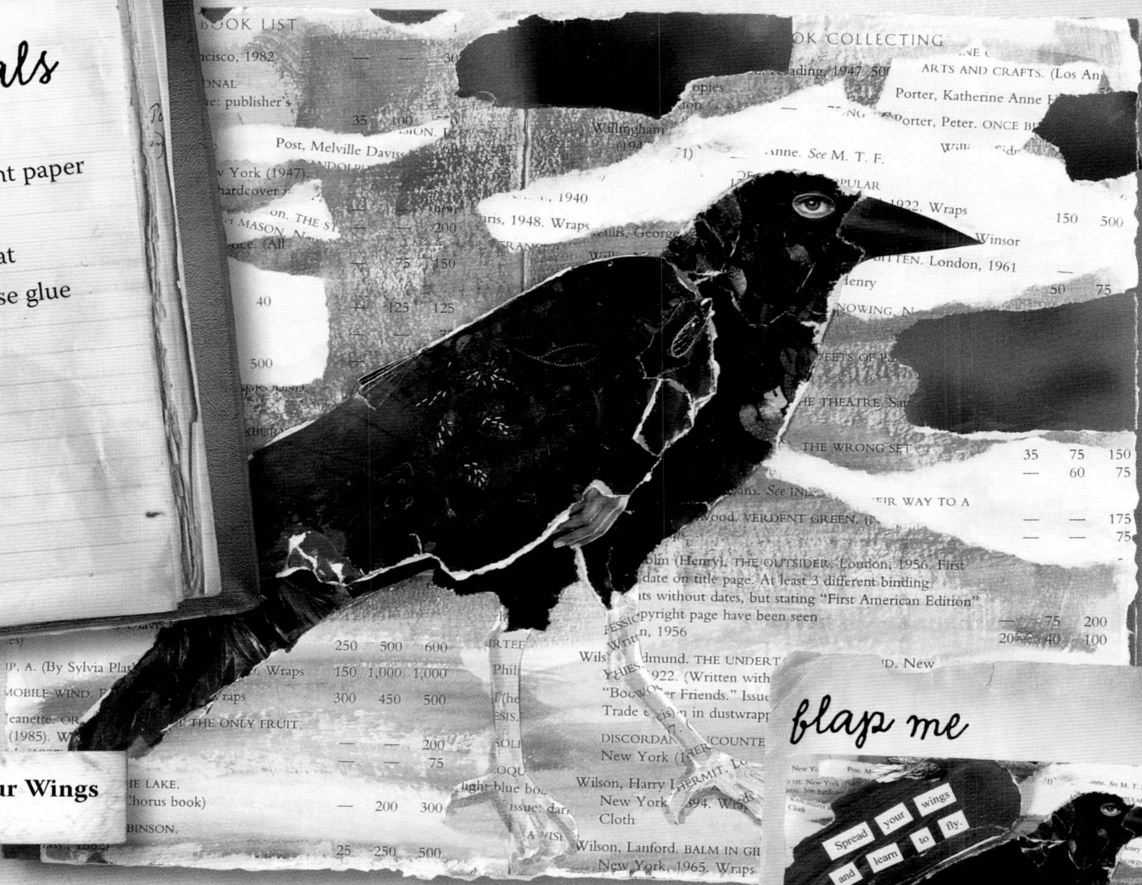

Spread Your Wings

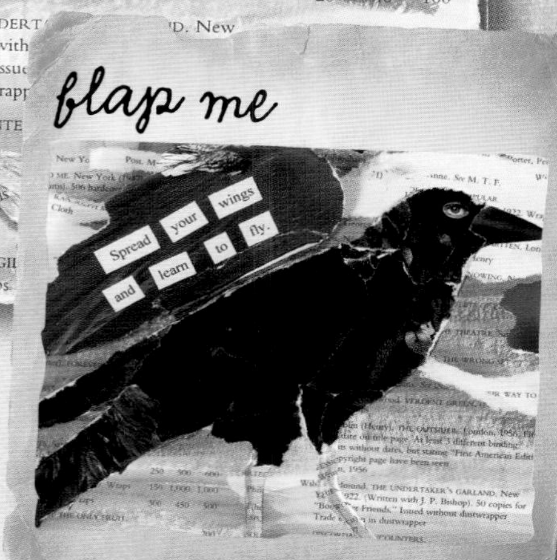

flap me

Spread your wings and learn to fly.

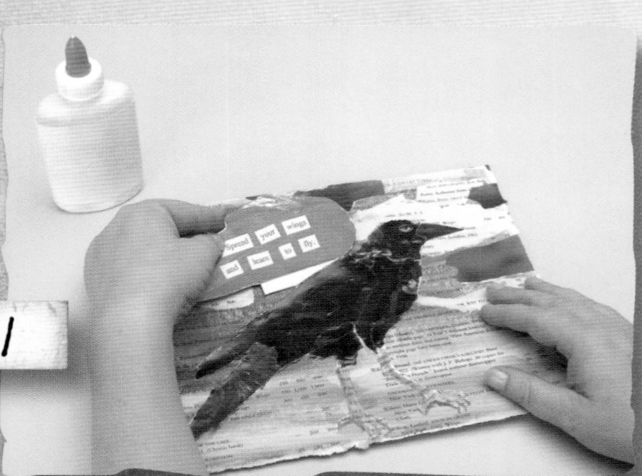

1

Create double-sided flap

Draw or adhere an existing image on both sides of a piece of heavyweight paper that will become your flap. When cutting the flap, include a tab where the flap will be inserted into the main image, as shown. Use a craft knife to cut a slit that's large enough to fit the tab in the main image. Apply all-purpose glue to the tab, insert it through the slot and adhere it to the back of your artwork.

Owls
Jan Drees

Fly Free
Joan Drees Lawrence

JANUARY
I bought the black telephone at our friend Art's auction. Running my finger along the rotary dial
I fingered the dial
I longed for one of my own and letting numbers dialing back
carry my finger back
682-9660
hang on me
Domino
PURE CANE
SUGAR

Hook and Line

This technique allows an image to be hung on a hook. When the image is not on the hook, it is kept attached to the background with a line. The interactive element of the design can be increased by creating imagery for the back of the hooked item. The example shown here also incorporates the wheel pivot by the use of a dial. Turn the dial to reveal a message to my Granny. Besides phone receivers, this technique lends itself to use with hands, hangers and shelves as the hook.

Materials

- image
- heavyweight paper
- cord, string, twine, etc.
- scissors
- all-purpose glue
- eyelet tool set and hammer

optional materials

- matte medium
- paintbrushes
- tape

1

Prepare background and create support

Draw, color, paint or collage a background image onto heavyweight paper. I used matte medium to collage pieces of a phone book and painted a phone onto heavyweight paper. Create your supporting piece (in this example, the cradle) to match the theme of the project. Use all-purpose glue to adhere the support piece, except for the top portion, and pull the top portion to the background, away from the background piece slightly to enable it to accept the hanging piece.

Create hanging piece and attach cord

Cut a piece of heavyweight paper to the size and shape you'd like your hanging piece to be, keeping in mind it needs to fit into the supporting piece you created in step 1 without slipping through it. Trace it on another piece of heavyweight paper and cut it out to make an identical piece. Collage, paint or decorate each piece however you choose; one will be the inside of the hanging piece, and one will be the outside. Glue the front and back pieces wrong sides together with the end of the line sandwiched between them.

Attach cord to project piece

Use an eyelet tool and hammer to create a hole on the project piece. Insert the line (curly shoelace) through the project piece. Flip the piece over and secure the line onto the back by tying a knot, adhering with all-purpose glue or a piece of tape. Embellish the project as desired.

Horse with no Name
Kim Rae Nugent

Eugene
Kim Rae Nugent

move me

It's the Journey

Image Slide

The mechanism for this technique is a paper disc that slides beneath a slot while the image rides above it. The image slide is a useful device for illustrating movement, a journey or a path in your artwork.

My dad, Ken, is the driver and inspiration for this piece. When I was a child we had a Volkswagen bug, and I have many happy memories of riding in that little car. I invite you to take your own trip down memory lane with this technique.

Materials

- image
- heavyweight paper
- craft knife
- cutting mat
- all-purpose glue
- eyelet
- eyelet tool set and hammer
- circle punch
- pencil or pen

optional materials

- map
- paintbrush
- gesso

Prepare background and cut path

Create or adhere a background onto heavyweight paper. I chose a piece of a map, then used a dry brush to apply gesso, so the image wasn't as prominent. Draw the path you want your image slide to travel. Use a craft knife to cut out an opening, approximately ¼" (6mm) wide along that line.

Make mechanism for image

Use a circle punch to cut 2 circles that are smaller than the image you want to move. Use an eyelet tool and a hammer to create a hole in the center of both circles. Place an eyelet through both holes, attaching the circles to each other. Flip the circles over and use an eyelet tool and a hammer to spread each eyelet back to secure them. Use all-purpose glue to adhere the image you want to move to the top of 1 of the circles.

The back view of the base attached to the image (car)

3. Place movable image

Use all-purpose glue to adhere your background to a backing sheet of heavyweight paper, keeping adhesive clear of the area within 1" (3cm) of the path cut in step 1. Gently lift 1 side of the path and slide the mechanism from step 2 so the path lays between the 2 circles of the mechanism. Repeat this for the other side of the path. The path should now act as a track for your movable image.

American Transport
Casey H. Nugent

It's You and Me
Kim Rae Nugent

spin me

Circle Flip

Sandwich a metal wire between two circles and...*voilà*... you can flip back and forth between the images. The beauty of this mechanism is that it allows both the front and back of the artwork to be utilized. Try using this technique to showcase close-up images of faces to illustrate different emotions or choices.

The inspiration for my piece began with a magazine image of Picasso's *The Kiss*. Using magazine images to work out the mechanism and then re-creating the project adding your own style gives a jump start to your design.

Materials

- images
- cardstock
- heavyweight paper
- 20-gauge wire [I used 8"–12" (20cm–31cm)]
- 2–4 spring clamps
- wire cutter
- glue stick
- circle punch (large enough to cut out faces)

1

Prepare background

Create your piece of art. Size the image on a computer or copier and print 2 copies of the art.

2

Assemble front panel

Cut different colors of cardstock in various widths. Use a glue stick to adhere the cardstock in layers to create a background. Use a glue stick to adhere the image on top of the cardstock background.

3

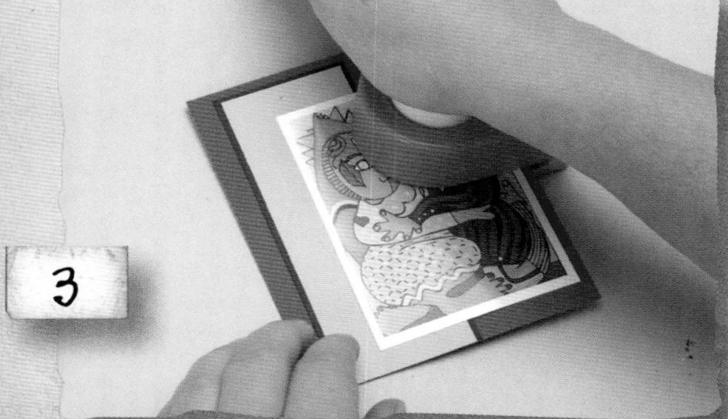

Punch hole in project

Take the panel piece from step 2 and center a paper punch over the part of the image you want to flip.

4

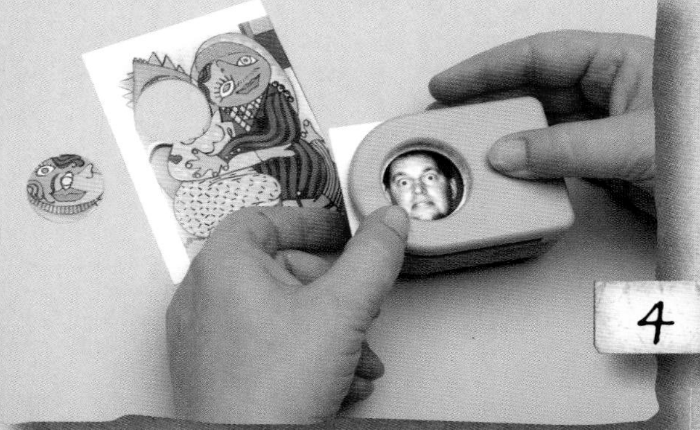

Create flip side

Punch out a different image to serve as the back of the punched-out image from step 3.

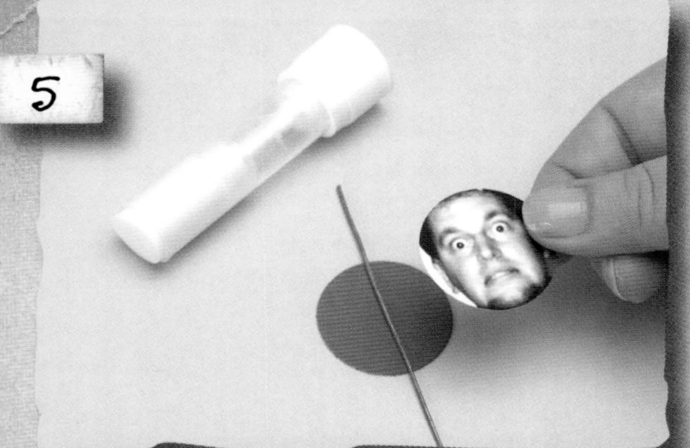

Attach images to wire

Cut a wire to a length 2" (5cm) longer than the diameter of the circle. Glue the 2 images for the rotating piece back-to-back with the wire centered between them. Make sure both images are oriented the same way. Use a spring clamp to hold them together until dry, if needed.

Create circle in back panel

Cut a piece of cardstock to the same size as the project; this will be your back panel. Lay the project on top of the back panel and trace the rotating piece onto the back panel. Line up the paper punch with the traced circle and punch a circle out of the back panel.

Apply backing

Place the rotating piece in the punched-out hole and use a glue stick to adhere the front panel to the back panel. The circle should flip between the images.

Design back panel

Remember, this can be a double-sided project. If you'd like, flip it over and add circles and quotes to the back panel. She loves me, she loves him...

A Vision from Afar
Casey H. Nugent

Sasquatch
Jill K. Berry

One Is Always Bigger
Tracie Lampe

Never Doubt a Mother's Love
Jodi Hollnagel-Jubran

Squeaker Mouse

Sound

If you've been in any stationery store lately, you've heard how popular greeting cards with sound have become. Here, I layered handmade paper to encase a squeaker inside a piece of artwork. The weight and flexibility of handmade paper makes it the perfect candidate for this project. You can use this technique to cover any number of sound elements, including bells and push-button music boxes.

Materials

- mat board or cardboard
- replaceable squeaker
- handmade paper
- spring clamps
- scissors
- all-purpose glue

optional materials

- dimensional items
- paint
- paintbrushes
- pencil

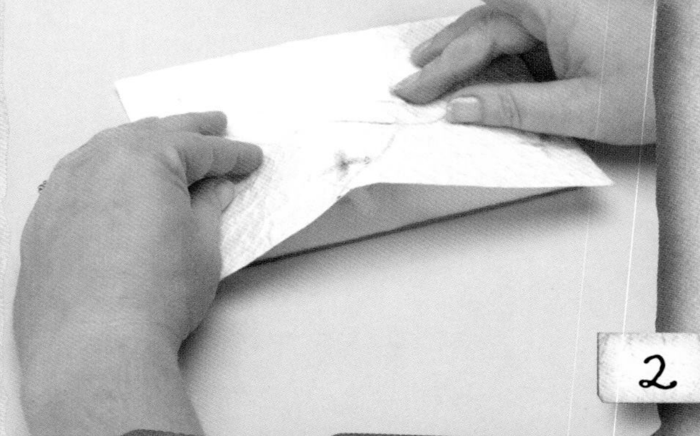

Apply glue and lay out squeaker

Cut a piece of cardboard or mat board to the desired size of the project. This will serve as the backing piece. Apply a thick coat of all-purpose glue to the entire surface of the cardboard. Position the squeaker so the stem overlaps 1 of the edges, enabling air to escape and make the noise.

Layer handmade paper

Cut a piece of handmade paper to a size slightly larger than the backing piece to allow room to cover the squeaker. Lay the handmade paper over the squeaker and backing. Use your fingers to press the handmade paper against the backing. Don't press it too snugly against the squeaker; the paper needs to be able to move. Allow this to dry. Use spring clamps to press together the edges to ensure that the paper dries flat.

3

Create image

Add any dimensional items to the project—here, I added ears.

4

Paint image

Paint, draw, color or collage the image you want on the front, positioning the area you want to squeak over the squeaker. Trim excess handmade paper.

Church Bells Package
Kim Rae Nugent

Pitter Patter
Jill K. Berry

Mermaid's Gift
Gina Louthian-Stanley

Tastes Her Palette

Tastes her palette.

smell me

Smell

When making your projects interactive, don't forget the power of smell. The oft-neglected olfactory sense evokes memories and emotions better than any of the other senses. Try this easy and inexpensive technique to make scratch-and-sniff art for all ages. Here I show you how to use unsweetened drink mixes, but you may also use various perfumes and spices, which are also excellent smell stimulators.

Materials

- heavyweight paper
- unsweetened powdered drink mix (makes 2 quarts)
- water
- large paintbrush
- mixing cup
- scissors
- glue stick

1

Mix and apply drink mix
Mix the contents of 1 package of the powdered drink mix with 1 teaspoon of water. Use a large paintbrush to apply your scented "paint" to a heavyweight paper. For best results, do this on a separate sheet of paper, not the actual project.

Stock up

Make extra scratch-and-sniff paper to use in future projects. After it has thoroughly dried, store it in a zippered plastic bag.

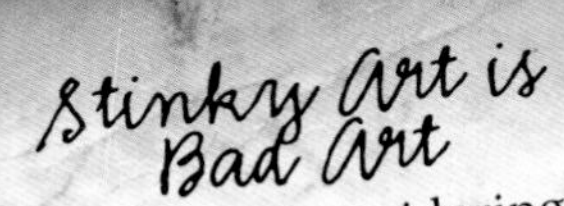

Stinky Art is Bad Art

Use care when considering perfume for art. Some people are allergic to certain perfumes.

2

Cut and apply shape
Cut out the shape of an object and use a glue stick to adhere it to the art. Smell the lemon lollipop!

Secrets of the Sea

Touch

Entice your audience to interact with your art by adding tactile elements. Layers of fiber, fabric and textures produce visual interest while beckoning to be touched. Analyze your projects to see where you can easily add touchable components. For animal subjects, try using feathers, faux fur or fabric. Sand and shells evoke the feel of the beach. Even a simple string that can be tied and untied gets the audience involved.

nce upon a time there was a far away land frozen with snow. The village was white and cold and the people who lived there were never comfortable. None of the clothes they wore kept them quite warm, none of the soup was hot enough to warm up their insides. Everyone was always on edge, unaware that there was any other way to live.

On a particularly bright white morning, a baby was born. She came into the world with her head up, and her eyes open. She saw the world with her first blink, and the people in the room saw her see it. She is so aware, they noticed. She is so alert they said. What does she see?

The baby grew quickly and took charge quickly. Everyone wanted to make her laugh, because when she did, they all felt a warm tingle that made them smile. The more she laughed, the warmer they got. She noticed everything around her and all that she saw made her happy. What does she see, the villagers wondered? What they saw was ice and snow, a landscape of dreary frozen whiteness.

Realm of the Ice Princess
Jill K. Berry

Life on Mars
Barbe Saint John

Colorful Characters
Kim Rae Nugent

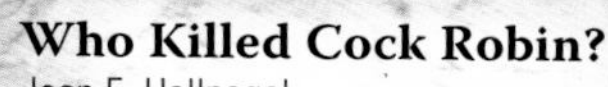

Who Killed Cock Robin?
Joan E. Hollnagel

Inspiration Gallery

Whether you're looking to make a piece about fishing interactive with a simple bit of string, as Sandra McCutcheon Pape did in *Gone Fishing* (page 113); or you're ready to layer hidden wonders in an intricate display as Jill Marie Shulse did in *Altered Amusements* (page 117), you're sure to find something to spark your creativity on the following pages.

Angel
Gwynn Thoma

Magic Brain Calculator
Kim Rae Nugent

Hawaii Book
Jill K. Berry

Chinese Butterfly
Deb Mortl

Pinwheels on Spools
Catherine Anderson

Greetings from Egypt
Barbe Saint John

Hot Mama
Jill K. Berry

Day at the Beach
Claudine Hellmuth

Game Boy
Gina Louthian-Stanley

A Window to My Creative Soul
Kim Rae Nugent

Gone Fishing
Sandra McCutcheon Pape

Gertie
Brook W. Berth

Family Portraits
Kim Rae Nugent

Who Killed Cock Robin?
Joan E. Hollnagel

Who killed Cock Robin?
I said the Sparrow,
With my bow and arrow,
I killed Cock Robin.

This is the Sparrow,
With his bow and arrow.

Behind Every Blossom
Cheryl Husmann

Beach Scene
Gwynn Thoma

Altered Souls
Lou McCulloch

Box
Jill K. Berry

Metamorphosis
Kim Rae Nugent

Altered Amusements
Jill Marie Shulse

Templates

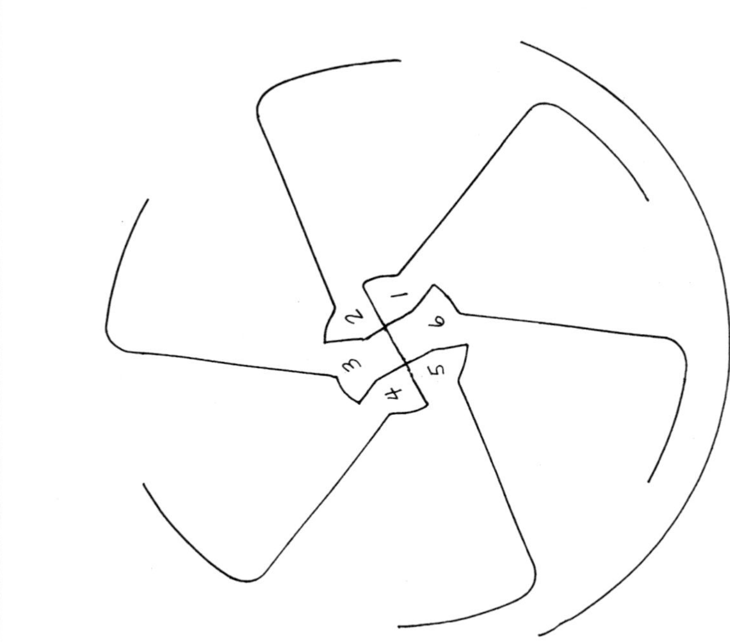

Revolving-Picture Tab template 1
(See page 68.)

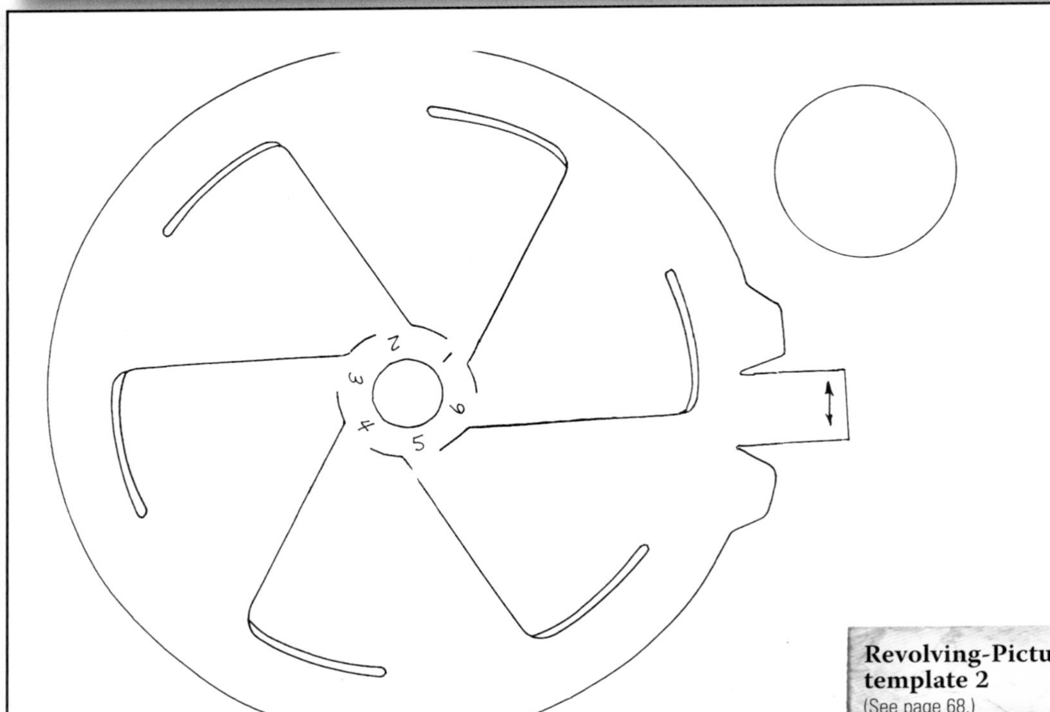

Revolving-Picture Tab template 2
(See page 68.)

Set photocopier to 200% to reproduce the template to the size I used; or, enlarge or reduce however you'd like for use in projects of your own.

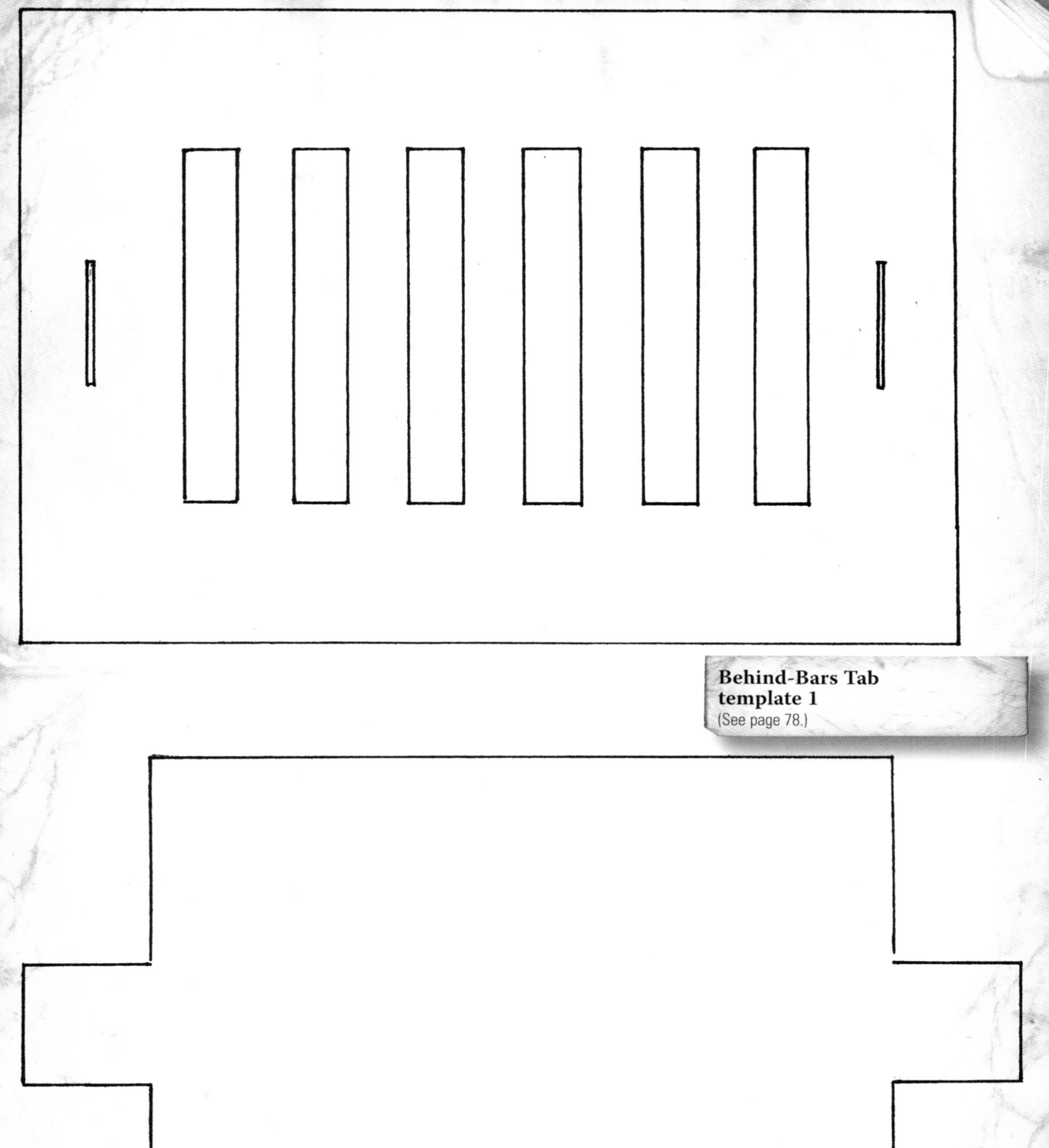

Behind-Bars Tab template 1
(See page 78.)

Set photocopier to 100% to reproduce the template to the size I used; or, enlarge or reduce however you'd like for use in projects of your own.

Behind-Bars Tab template 2
(See page 78.)

About the Contributing Artists

I asked each of the contributing artists to create an interactive self-portrait ATC. Peruse the following pages to learn a little about your favorite artists—and see how much fun you can have using just 2½" × 3½" (6cm × 9cm) of material.

Catherine Anderson

Catherine is a photographer and mixed-media artist who was born in South Africa. She was an attorney for fourteen years before moving to the United States with her family and starting a new career as an artist. She particularly loves to play and teach in any art medium that involves visual images. She's also a SoulCollage facilitator (www.soulcollage.com). She uses her photography to bring attention to the challenges faced by AIDS orphans in South Africa. Catherine resides in Charlotte, North Carolina.

cathy@catherineandersonstudio.com
www.catherineandersonstudio.com

Rita Bellanca

Rita started dabbling in art five years ago, after years of believing that if you weren't born with a paintbrush in your hand, there was no point in trying. Thankfully, she discovered the wonders of online art groups and became addicted to art swaps. Rita says, "Swaps fueled my love of experimentation, and the support I received as a newbie helped boost my confidence." She particularly enjoys digital collage but loves experimenting with just about every medium under the sun. Rita resides in Seattle, Washington.

discodog01@hotmail.com
atomicwarbride.blogspot.com

Jill K. Berry

Jill is an artist, teacher and mom who makes lots of books and paintings and anything else that strikes her fancy. Born and raised in California, she also spent a year studying art in Italy, where she learned to see a bigger picture of art and the world in general. She focuses her work on content and color; it often involves maps, symbols, houses, housewives and the mystique of charisma. You can see her work in *Letter Arts Review*, *Somerset Studio* and various other publications. Her work is also in public and private collections throughout the United States. Jill resides in the foothills of the Rocky Mountains.

jill@jillberrydesign.com
www.jillberrydesign.com

Brook W. Berth

Brook is a mixed-media artist. She attended the University of Wisconsin–Oshkosh with a major in graphic design. In addition to working as a graphic artist for *Sailing Magazine*, Brook runs a home-based sign and design firm, Gunther Graphics, named after her Boston terrier. She's worked for clients ranging from magazines and newspapers to individuals, small businesses and corporations in just about every genre. She's done everything from branding, creating logos and identities, to print, Web signage and monument design. *Layers* magazine chose Brook to create a design makeover for their July/August 2006 issue. Brook describes her design style as eclectic and streamlined with an urban flair. Brook currently resides in Jackson, Wisconsin, with her husband, Joel, and their dogs.
brook@gunthergraphics.com
www.gunthergraphics.com

Hope M. Clinchot

Hope is a self-taught artist who, for as long as she can remember, has loved to create things. Starting in early childhood, Hope loved to draw dancing figures in big puffy ball gowns, assemble "nature people" from leaves and twigs and, of course, make her own doll furniture and clothing! Today she works mostly in mixed media, because she "never wants to limit [her] choices for creativity." She is inspired by color and odd, whimsical things that make her take a second look. Hope resides in Portsmouth, Virginia.
gabbihope@hotmail.com

Jan Drees

Jan Drees has worked more than thirty years as a woodcarver. For the last fifteen years, she's made concrete sculptures, and somewhere in there she started working in mixed media, jewelry, dolls and more. Because she earns a living working full-time as an artist, Jan keeps challenging herself to new mediums. She is mostly self-taught but has taken private lessons from some master sculptors. Jan's artwork has appeared in *Art Doll Quarterly*. She is now involved in product development, working with different craft manufacturers. Jan resides in Elkhart Lake, Wisconsin.
skulpter@msn.com
www.jandreesart.com

Claudine Hellmuth

Claudine is a nationally recognized collage artist, author and illustrator. She combines photos, paint, paper and pen into quirky, whimsical-retro collages that she calls Poppets. Her art has been featured on *The Martha Stewart Show*, in Mary Engelbreit's *Home Companion* magazine, on HGTV's *I Want That!* and on the DIY Network program *Craft Lab*. In addition to creating her artwork full-time, Claudine teaches collage workshops in the United States and Canada. She's written two North Light Books, *Collage Discovery Workshop* and *Collage Discovery Workshop: Beyond the Unexpected*. She has also produced three instructional DVD workshops. Claudine resides in Washington, D.C., with her husband, Paul, and their very spoiled pets, a dog and two cats..
www.collageartist.com

Joan E. Hollnagel

Joan is an active member of the Cedarburg Artists Guild. She is a mixed-media artist whose whimsical style delights young and old alike. She is an accomplished painter and sculptor who has exhibited at local and national levels, and her art has received several awards and purchase prizes. Joan resides in Cedarburg, Wisconsin.
artistjoan@sbcglobal.net
www.joanhollnagel.com

Jodi Hollnagel-Jubran

Jodi received her bachelor of fine arts from the University of Wisconsin–Milwaukee and her master of fine arts from East Carolina University in sculpture. She and her husband, Hanna Jubran, own and operate J&H Studio, Inc. They teach at East Carolina University, make and exhibit their art, and travel the world participating in international sculpture symposiums. Some of her featured works include: a bronze eagle with a 22' (7m) wingspan for The Jesse Helms Center in Wingate, North Carolina; an 11' (3m) bronze wildcat at Davidson College in Davidson, North Carolina; a 12' (4m) bronze Scotsman at Presbyterian College in Clinton, South Carolina; a 13' (4m) bronze pirate at East Carolina University in Greenville, North Carolina; and *A Monument to a Century of Flight* in Kitty Hawk, North Carolina.
jodihollnageljubran.com

Cheryl Husmann

Cheryl is a mixed-media artist with a penchant for paper and all things vintage. Collage, small books and scrapbooking are now the main focus of her artistic endeavors. Her goal is always to capture the past and the present, and to preserve it for the future. Currently an artist-on-call for Stampington & Co., she produces samples for their line of art stamps. Her papercrafts have been published in various issues of *Somerset Studio, Stampers' Sampler, ATCs: An Anthology, Transparent Art* and *Handcrafted.* Cheryl resides in the small town of Grafton, Wisconsin, just north of Milwaukee.
cheryl_husmann@yahoo.com

Tracie Lampe

Tracie is a self-taught artist who has found that creating things really feeds her soul! Tracie's medium of choice is fiber, but she loves trying all mediums. Tracie resides in Michigan with her wonderful hubby, two fabulous children and two dogs.
TLampe@LampesLumps.com.
www.LampesLumps.com
www.lampeslumps.typepad.com

Joan Drees Lawrence

A full-time nurse by day and a self-taught mixed-media artist by night, Joan's love for paper and the printing process has progressed to a love for found objects and ephemera. She spends her free time creating collages, ATCs and shrines. Joan has participated in more than 150 swaps including chunky books, banners and altered arts. Her art has been featured on several faux postage sheets at ARTchixstudio. Joan resides in Sheboygan, Wisconsin.
rsjoan@gmail.com

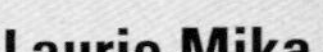

Gina Louthian-Stanley

Gina is a teacher, writer, workshop instructor, monotype printmaker, collage artist and jewelry maker. Her intrinsic artistic talent appeared around the age of eighteen months when she began scribbling colorful imagery on her bedroom walls, and later carved designs and cryptic messages on her parents' fine furniture. She has been creating art ever since. Gina earned her bachelor of arts degree at Hollins University and her master's degree at Radford University. Gina resides in the beautiful Blue Ridge Mountains of Virginia.
lougael@cox.net

Lou McCulloch

As a former magazine senior designer, Lou tries to keep up on the latest art trends. She almost always uses vintage ephemera in her art because of her life-long interest in the subject. A few years ago, she became interested in combining found objects and antique photographs with her ephemera. Some of Lou's work can be seen in the North Light Book *Kaleidoscope.* Her work has also been showcased in the magazines *Somerset Studio, Artitude, Altered Arts* and *Cloth Paper Scissors.* She continues to build assemblages, as well as other mixed-media works. Lou resides in Medina, Ohio.
metamorphosis.typepad.com/metamorphosis
www.cafepress.com/glimpses

Laurie Mika

Laurie is a mixed-media artist with a passion for combining and overlapping a variety of mediums, creating an original style of mixed-media mosaics and assemblage using handmade tiles. Laurie's love of travel to far-off places and her experiences living in East Africa have shaped the way her art looks today. Her work is embellished with the many little treasures found during her travels. Laurie teaches at nationally recognized art retreats, and her mixed-media mosaics have been included in many group shows, galleries and private collections. Her work has also been published in several Stampington & Co. magazines and other publications. She was featured on HGTV's *Crafters Coast to Coast* and on DIY network's *Craft Lab.* Laurie is also the author of the North Light Book, *Mixed-Media Mosaics.*
www.mikaarts.com
laurie@mikaarts.com

Deb Mortl

Deb is an oil painter whose work focuses primarily on the textural and color properties of the country landscape. She often incorporates collage into her pieces by adding another layer of pattern or texture into the painting. Her work is on display in numerous galleries, and she is represented by Fine Line Designs Gallery in Ephraim, Wisconsin (www.finelinedesignsgallery.com). Deb is a graduate of the Milwaukee Institute of Art and Design. She resides in Mequon, Wisconsin, where she teaches at a local high school.
artistpunk@gmail.com

Casey H. Nugent

Casey is an industrial designer who received his bachelor of fine arts from the University of Wisconsin–Stout. Casey has mechanical aptitude along with creative problem-solving skills, as evidenced in his art and design where he combines form and function. His other strong suits include model making, sketching and computer modeling and rendering.
www.caseynugent.com

Sandra McCutcheon Pape

Sandra is a painter, jeweler and mixed-media collage and assemblage artist. She is a collector and gatherer of found objects that have a past and a history. She creates her art from these objects and collections. For Sandra, art and collecting go hand-in-hand; they work together, feed off one another, and are necessary components that enhance the creative process for making art. Her artwork challenges the viewer to think in a nonlinear fashion, as in a dream. Her process is intuitive, and her art is intensely personal. She has been in numerous juried shows and is represented in Wisconsin galleries. Living in an 1863 fieldstone farm house, and working in her third-floor studio in a restored 1864 Woolen Mill, she is warmly embraced by history and art. Sandra resides in historic Cedarburg, Wisconsin, with her husband.
smpape@msn.com

Cris Peacock

Cris is an artist and art educator. Her first commission came during the fifth grade when her school principal asked her to paint a 5' × 20' (2m × 6m) mural of the United States on the blacktop outside his office. Since then, Cris has enjoyed painting murals on buildings, driveways and swimming pools. Her love of the sea and nature is seen in much of the work she creates. Cris lives in Ma'alaea, Maui, Hawaii, with her true love, Phil, and her needy cat. She spends her time exploring all types of media, sharing art with others and visiting her grown children on the mainland.
www.crispart.net

Barbe Saint John

Barbe is a mostly self-taught mixed-media artist. Her work is primarily about alchemy—the transmutation of common, obscure and abandoned items into objects with value and meaning. She loves the challenge of making something from nothing. Barbe explores many different art mediums, but currently she can be found spinning weird novelty yarns, crafting assemblages and reliquaries or fabricating found-object jewelry. Barbe lives in San Francisco, California, with her husband, spoiled Chihuahua and herd of bad cats.
www.barbesaintjohn.com
www.barbesaintjohn.blogspot.com

Jill Marie Shulse

Jill is a self-taught mixed-media artist who enjoys creating altered assemblages and jewelry, and incorporating found objects into her artwork. She was an artist-on-call for Stampington's & Co.'s *Inspirations* magazine, and has also had her work published in *Belle Armoire, Belle Armoire Jewelry, Legacy, Somerset Home, Altered Couture, Haute Handbags, Stamper's' Sampler, Somerset Studio* and *Somerset Workshop*. Jill resides in rural Hingham, Wisconsin, with her husband, daughter and three adorable pugs.
jillstng@wi.rr.com
www.jillmarieshulse.blogspot.com

Paula Strains

Paula studied weaving and fabric painting at the University of Wisconsin–Milwaukee and at the Beijing School of Arts and Crafts in China, earning a bachelor of fine arts degree. She designed and taught the art curriculum for primary school students on St. Kitts, in the West Indies, with the U.S. Peace Corps. Paula currently paints in acrylics and draws with ink, colored pencils and pastels. Most recently, she worked as a graphic designer for *Sailing Magazine*.
pastrains@gmail.com

Gwynn Thoma

Gwynn enjoys all forms of art, including altered books and journals, quilting collage, pique assiette and knitting. Gwynn has been published in *Somerset Studio, Belle Armoire* and *Haute Handbags*. She resides in the Sierra Mountains in Twain Harte, California.
gwynnthoma@goldrush.com

Judy Wise

Judy Wise has worked as a printmaker and painter for nearly three decades and has kept daily journals of her writing and art since before the age of ten. Her work has been featured on greeting cards and has been published in books, magazines, calendars, educational materials and on tapestries. She is a passionate lover of all things artful and of helping others find joy in the process of self-expression. She believes making art is an innately human trait and that everyone is creative. Judy resides in Oregon.
www.judywise.com
judywise@canby.com

Resources

Art Supplies

Art Supply Warehouse
An online store and catalog with a large selection of art supplies, including oil paint sticks
5325 Departure Dr.
Raleigh, NC 27616-1835
(800) 995-6778
www.aswexpress.com

Century Novelty Company, Inc.
An online store with craft supplies, including puzzles
38239 Plymouth Rd.
Livonia, Michigan 48150-1051
(800) 325-6232
www.centurynovelty.com

Cloth Paper Scissors
A magazine and online store
P.O. Box 685
Stow, MA 01775
(866) 698-6989
www.clothpaperscissors.com

Oriental Trading Company, Inc.
A catalog and online store with craft supplies and puzzles
P.O. Box 2308
Omaha, Nebraska 68103-0407
(800) 875-8480
www.orientaltrading.com

Stampington & Company
A great resource for inspirational books, magazines and art supplies
22992 Mill Creek, Suite B
Laguna Hills, CA 92653
(877) STAMPER
www.somersetstudio.com

Tools

Harbor Freight
A retail, online store and catalog with a large selection of tools
3491 Mission Oaks Blvd.
Camarillo, CA 93011
(800) 444-3353
www. harborfreight.com

S&J's Discount Tools
An online store with a large selection of tools, including gasket punch sets
2892 Prairie Dr.
Lewis Center, OH 43035
www.sjdiscounttools.com

Paper Engineers

Mark Hiner
A talented paper engineer with an informative Web site that includes a history of interactive art
www.markhiner.co.uk

Joan Irvine
Called the pop-up lady by children, her Web site features her books and shows you how to create pop-ups
www.makersgallery.com/joanirvine

Robert Sabuda
An amazing paper engineer who features projects on his Web site
www.robertsabuda.com

Organizations

Cedarburg Artists Guild
Dedicated to promoting and preserving the arts in Southeastern Wisconsin through education, scholarships, events and programs
P.O. Box 663
Cedarburg, WI 53012
www.cedarburgartistsguild.com

The Cedarburg Cultural Center
A unique blend of a performing-arts center, art gallery and education facility, museum and community gathering place
W62 N546 Washington Ave.
Cedarburg, WI 53012
www.cedarburgculturalcenter.org

Ozaukee Art Center
A fine-arts complex featuring exhibitions and workshops in all media, including the Sculpture Studio of Paul J. Yank
W62 N718 Riveredge Dr.
Cedarburg, WI 53012
(262) 377-8230

Art Retreat

RAEvN's Nest Art Retreat
An annual retreat to nourish your creative soul, located in a quaint historic Midwest town
Cedarburg, Wisconsin
www.raevns-nest-art-retreat.com

Index

Set your creativity in motion with these other North Light Books.

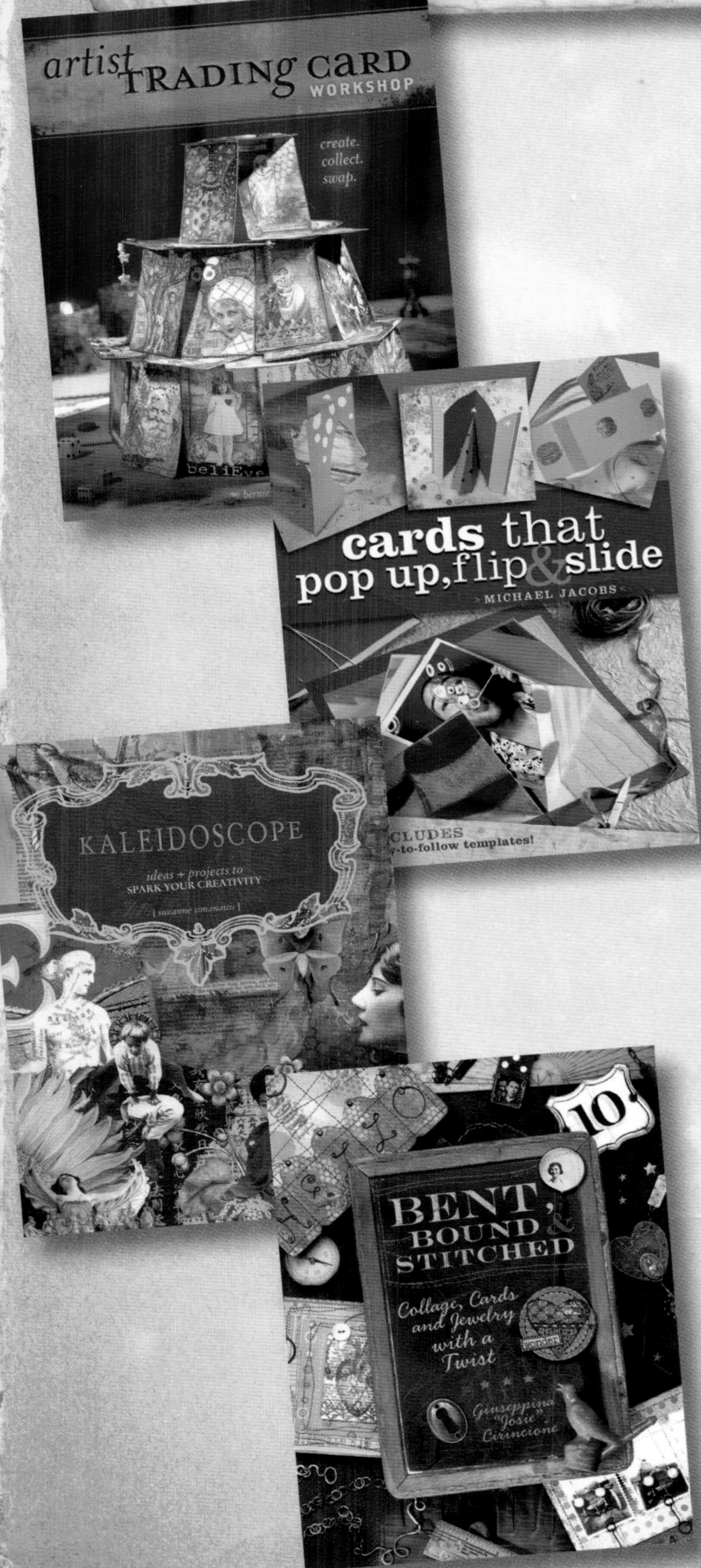

Artist Trading Cards Workshop

Bernie Berlin

Find instruction and ideas for using a variety of mediums to make artist trading cards to collect and swap. Whatever your crafting background, you'll find innovative techniques for making ATCs, including collage, painting, metal working, stamping and more. The book even offers suggestions for starting your own artistic community to trade techniques and cards.
ISBN-10: 1-58180-848-8, ISBN-13: 978-1-58180-848-3
paperback, 128 pages, Z0524

Cards that Pop-Up, Flip and Slide

Michael Jacobs

Learn how to craft one-of-a-kind, dynamic, interactive cards with moving parts such as pop-ups, sliders and flaps. Choose from 22 step-by-step projects that use a variety of papers—from handmade and printed to recycled—to create unique graphic looks. Then create coordinating envelopes to complete the look of your card.
ISBN 1-58180-596-9, ISBN-13 978-1-58180-596-3
paperback, 96 pages, 33109

Kaleidoscope

Suzanne Simanaitis

Kaleidoscope delivers your creative muse directly to your workspace. Featuring interactive and energizing creativity prompts ranging from inspiring stories to personality tests, doodle exercises, purses in duct tape and a cut-and-fold shrine, this is one-stop shopping for getting your creative juices flowing. The book showcases eye candy artwork and projects with instruction from some of the hottest collage, mixed-media and altered artists.
ISBN-10: 1-58180-879-8, ISBN-13: 978-1-58180-879-7
paperback, 144 pages, Z0346

Bent, Bound & Stitched

Giuseppina Cirincione

Collage, cards and jewelry with a twist! This book is full of techniques that any aspiring artist will love. Learn to bend and shape wire into letter and number embellishments, use a sewing wheel and acrylic paint to add texture to papers, make hinges from a portion of a rubber stamp, add texture to cards with basic sewing, combine rivets and shrink plastic, and more!
ISBN-10: 1-60061-060-9, ISBN-13: 978-1-60061-060-8
paperback, 128 pages, Z1752

These and other fine North Light Books are available at your local craft retailer, bookstore or online supplier, or visit our Web site at **www.mycraftivity.com**.